Palliative and Terminal Care

Health Care Needs Assessment

the epidemiologically based needs assessment reviews

Second series

WB310

Edited by

Andrew Stevens

Professor of Public Health Medicine, The University of Birmingham

(formerly Senior Lecturer in Public Health Medicine,
The Wessex Institute for Health Research and Development)

and

James Raftery

Professor of Health Economics,
Health Services Management Centre
The University of Birmingham

(formerly Senior Health Economist,
The Wessex Institute for Health Research and Development)

Produced by

for Health Research & Development
incorporating Public Health Medicine

RADCLIFFE MEDICAL PRESS
OXFORD and NEW YORK

Radcliffe Medical Press Ltd
18 Marcham Road, Abingdon, Oxon OX14 1AA, UK

Radcliffe Medical Press, Inc.
141 Fifth Avenue, New York, NY 10010, USA

British Library Cataloguing in Publication Data

A cataloguing record for this book is available from the British Library.

ISBN 1 85775 206 6

Library of Congress Cataloging-in-Publication Data is available.

Typeset by Tradespools Ltd, Frome, Somerset
Printed and bound in Great Britain by Redwood Books, Trowbridge, Wiltshire

Contents

Introduction
A Stevens, J Raftery

Palliative and Terminal Care
I Higginson

Foreword

Everyone involved in the purchasing, planning and prioritization of health care needs accurate, comprehensive and well-packaged information to answer at least four crucial questions. With what population or patients are we concerned? What services are provided? What is the evidence of the effectiveness of services? What is the optimum set of services? In other words: What is the need and how can it be best met?

These questions are answered in part by epidemiological literature and in part by the products of the evidence-based health care movement. The *Health Care Needs Assessment* series neatly combines these two elements and offers a perspective across an entire disease or service area. A purchaser or practitioner reading one of these chapters is rapidly brought up-to-speed with the whole spectrum of care.

Many positive comments, including evidence supplied to the House of Commons' Health Committee, have demonstrated the value and importance of the first series. The additional topics in the second series extend the range of information available covering both areas where the assessment of need and effectiveness of services has long been discussed, such as aspects of gynaecology and low back pain, and ones in which there has been less interest, such as dermatology. The new series will be welcomed by purchasers of health care in the United Kingdom but it should also be of value to all those concerned with assessing and meeting health care needs, from central government to individual practitioners.

Graham Winyard
Medical Director, NHS Executive
September 1996

Preface

This book forms part of the second series of health care needs assessment reviews. The first series, published in 1994, comprises reviews of 20 diseases, interventions or services selected for their importance to purchasers of health care. Importance is defined in terms of burden of disease (mortality, morbidity and cost), the likely scope for changing patterns of purchasing and the wish to see a wide range of topics to test the method used for needs assessment. The first series also includes an introductory chapter, explaining the background to needs assessment and a conclusive chapter, bringing together the main findings of the disease reviews.

The eight reports have been chosen, using the same importance criteria to increase the coverage of all health service activity. There has been a small change in emphasis, away from disease groups (strictly *Breast Cancer* only), to services and in some cases entire specialties (*Dermatology* and *Gynaecology*). The change has been partly to maintain coverage of substantial areas in each report (where otherwise a relatively small disease group would now require an individual chapter) and also to reflect the wishes of the users for the topic areas to be consistent with the scope of purchasing plans if at all possible.

As before the authors have been selected on the basis of academic expertise and each chapter is the work of individual authors. The reviews do not necessarily reflect the views of the National Health Service Executive that sponsored the project, nor indeed the current professional consensus. Each review should be in no way regarded as setting norms; rather it should be used as a valuable source of evidence and arguments on which purchasing authorities may base their decisions.

There have been other changes since the first series which have influenced the range of reviews and the content of individual reviews. First districts have merged and a population base of 250 000 is no longer the norm. Denominators are now expressed as per 100 000, or per million population. Second the term purchasers no longer strictly means just district health authorities. Some small steps have therefore been taken in the direction of making the material relevant to primary care purchasing. This is particularly so in the *Low Back Pain* review, in which the focus is on the presenting symptom as in general practice rather than on a confirmed diagnosis following secondary care. Third the science of systematic reviews and meta-analyses has developed remarkably since the production of the first series. While this important development has been of great use to purchasers, the role of the needs assessment in covering entire disease and service areas remains unique. Both objectives of providing baseline information for purchasers to assist with the knowledge-base of all the processes around purchasing and designing a method for needs assessment have largely been vindicated by comments received on the first series and the demand for a second series.

The editors wish to acknowledge the contribution of those who helped with the origination of the project: Graham Winyard, Mike Dunning, Deirdre Cunningham and Azim Lakhani; and also members of the current Steering Group: Mark Charny, Anne Kauder and Graham Bickler; as well as those at Wessex who have enabled the project to run smoothly: Ros Liddiard, Pat Barrett and Melanie Corris.

Contributing author

Higginson, Professor I
Department of Palliative Care and Policy
The Rayne Institute
King's College School of Medicine and Dentistry
Bessemer Road
LONDON SE5 9PJ

Introduction

A Stevens, J Raftery

Needs assessment means different things according to who uses the term, when and where. Some of these uses are reviewed in this introduction. Our understanding of needs assessment stems from the wish to provide useful information for those involved in the priority setting and purchasing of health care.

We are concerned with population health care need and define it as 'the population's ability to benefit from health care'[1,2,3] as did Culyer 20 years ago.[4] Mention of health care is important because for the purposes of commissioning health services it is crucial that there be some benefit from the interventions that follow from the assessment of need. The benefit can be immediate or in the future, physical or psychological, personal or communal. The intervention can concern health promotion, diagnosis, or palliation as well as treatment. We argue that needs are worth assessing when something useful can be done about them. The two essential determinants of a population's ability to benefit are the:

- incidence and/or prevalence of a health problem
- effectiveness of the interventions available to deal with it.

These two components form the core of the protocol used in the chapters that follow.

Current service provision although not a determinant of need is also highly relevant if needs assessment is to have any value in action. We need to know how things stand before we can change them. The reliance of our approach on these three elements is shown in Figure 1. The effectiveness corner of the triangle includes *cost*-effectiveness because this allows us to consider the *relative* priority of different needs.

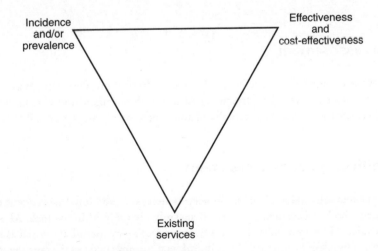

Figure 1: The elements of health care needs assessment.

We also distinguish need from demand (what people would be willing to pay for or might wish to use in a system of free health care) and from supply (what is actually provided).[1,2,3] This helps to classify health service interventions according to whether they reflect need, demand or supply (or some combination). It also highlights the need for caution in the use of information sources which often say more about supply (e.g. utilization rates) or demand (e.g. patient preference surveys) than they do about need. It also reminds health care commissioners of the importance of drawing together needs, supply and demand as shown in Figure 2. The central area of overlap is the optimum field for service provision, i.e. where need, supply and demand are congruent.

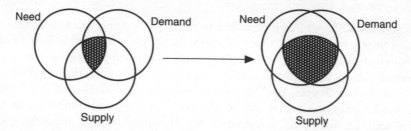

Figure 2: Drawing need, demand and supply together: the role of the purchasers of health care.

We also suggest three practical tools for health care needs assessment (see page xvi):

1   epidemiological
2   comparative
3   corporate.

Alternative approaches

There is a considerable range of alternative approaches to needs assessment depending on their purpose and context.

Social services assessment

In UK public policy the community care reforms which have stressed individual needs assessment for social care. Local authority social services departments must assess the needs of individuals for personal social services that mainly cover the elderly, the mentally ill and people with learning disabilities.[5]

Individual health care needs assessment

In health care too, the mentally ill have become subject to increased individual assessment through the care programme approach which is designed to cover all severely mentally ill individuals who are about to be discharged from hospital.[6] However individual health care needs assessment has existed as long as medicine and is the key feature of much of health care. The clinical focus regards need as the best that can be done for a patient in a particular setting. In primary care the establishment of routine health checks in the UK, especially for the over 75s, is an example of formalized individual needs assessment, which raised controversy in its imposition of mass individual needs assessment that includes people who are not necessarily in any need.[7,8]

Participatory priority setting

In the US needs assessment is often used as a term for participatory priority setting by organizations, which are usually public sector or voluntary rather than for profit. These involve three elements: defining the needs of organizations or groups, setting priorities and democratic involvement.[9] At state level the now famous Oregon approach to priority setting has much in common with needs assessment for health care commissioning in the UK but the explicit use of the participatory democratic element in the US was striking.[10] Even in the UK health policy since 1991 has attributed growing importance to the role of the public. This has been both in the form of central exhortation[11,12] and in local practice as many district health authorities have tried to involve the public in priority setting.[13] Public involvement has also occurred unintentionally through the media: a series of controversial cases, notably Child B who was denied a second NHS funded bone marrow transplant for leukaemia on the basis of the likely ineffectiveness of the treatment, have raised national debates.[14]

Primary care approaches

Other approaches, some imposed from above and some experimental from below are emerging from attempts to establish needs assessment in primary care. The routine assessment of the over 75s is an example of a top-down initiative and is unusual in requiring individual needs assessment by general practitioners of an entire age group.[7,8] Bottom-up experimental approaches tend to be based around data gathering through different means including for example rapid participatory appraisal, the analysis of routinely available small area statistics and the collation of practice-held information.[15,16] The analysis of small area statistics has a long tradition, including the use of Jarman indicators[17] and belongs to the comparative method of health care needs assessment – principally identifying a need for further analysis. Examining practice-held information including the audit of general practice case notes has had a growing role and is potentially much more relevant to population needs assessment than audit in secondary care. Because primary care case notes have a wide population coverage (90% of a practice population in three years) and each primary health care team has a relatively small population, it is possible for a primary health care team to expose practice population needs (given a knowledge of the effectiveness of interventions) through case note analysis. The development of computerized case notes in general practice could dramatically increase the scope for this approach.

Local surveys

In health authorities the use of local surveys has increased. These can cover multiple client groups and involve the collection of objective morbidity data. Local bespoke surveys of morbidity[18] can be supplemented by the interpretation of semi-routine data from national surveys such as the General Household Survey[19] and the OPCS Disability Survey.[20,21] Directors of Public Health annual health reports often include both local surveys and elements of such data. These can collect valuable information, although there is a risk that when local surveys are both limited to a selective range of client groups, and are centred around subjective information, they will give disproportionate importance to a selective range of interests.

Specialty-specific documents

Documents setting out the service requirements of client groups of an individual specialty are sometimes also treated as needs assessments. These often recommend the augmentation of services (within that specialty). Their validity as needs assessment documents depends on the explicitness and thoroughness of their research base.

Clinical effectiveness research

Finally, perhaps the most important contribution to needs assessment has been the major expansion of clinical effectiveness research in the UK and elsewhere. In the UK the Department of Health's research programme and especially its emphasis on 'health technology assessment' is a major attempt to evaluate the effectiveness of many health care interventions and therefore inform the health care needs which underlie them.[22,23]

In determining the differences between these various approaches to needs assessment it is helpful to ask the following questions:

1 **Is the principal concern with health or social services?** The effectiveness component of need for social services is often not recognized. The reason for this may be that there is seldom a clear-cut distinction between what works and what does not. More housing or more education is seldom seen as undesirable. In health care, by contrast, some interventions work spectacularly well but a point arises at which increased intervention *is* undesirable. Excessive medication or surgery may not only be of no benefit but can be harmful. It could be argued that in social care the potential open-endedness of benefit and therefore of spending makes it more important to assess the effectiveness of interventions and make a judgement of what the need is. The spectre of rationing in a politically charged context often deters such explicitness.

2 **Is the needs assessment about population or individuals?** Many approaches to needs assessment are necessarily concerned with individuals. Local authority social services programmes and primary care health checks focus on individuals. Traditional clinical decision making and also some purchasing decisions such as extra-contractual referrals concern individuals. The media focus is almost always on the individual. Although individual needs assessment can be seen as the opposite end of the spectrum from population based needs assessment the underlying logic is the same.

The purchaser (population needs assessor) is concerned with meeting the aggregate needs of the population. For some client groups where individuals are either few or prominent in their health care costs, such as in the case of mentally disordered offenders they may well need to be individually counted or even individually assessed to provide the population picture.[24,25] Wing *et al.* consider the purchaser's population view and the individual clinical view of mental health need to be 'largely identical'.[26] In part they say this because individual needs can be aggregated but in part they recognize the importance of service effectiveness as integral to the need equation.

3 **Is there a clear context of allocating scarce resources?** Needs assessments that fail to acknowledge resource limitations are common but are of restricted value to health care commissioners. This can be a problem with individual clinical needs assessment, which can put great pressure on health budgets and squeeze the care available to patients with weak advocates. However clinicians work within an (often) implicit resource framework. Population health care needs assessment makes that framework explicit. Some population approaches also fail to acknowledge resource issues. This can be a problem with population surveys if they are neither set in the context of effectiveness, nor make it clear that they are

exploratory. It is also a difficulty with specialty-specific documents recommending levels of service within the specialty.[27] Examples abound as many specialties are anxious to protect or enhance the resources available to them.[28] This may be justified but they risk being little more than a group extension of an unbounded clinical decision making procedure.

4   **Is the needs assessment about priority setting within the context of a variety of competing needs or is it about advocacy for a single group or individual?** This is closely related to the resource context question. Specialty-specific documents, client group surveys and even policy directives which focus on single groups often represent advocacy rather than balanced contributions to priority setting. Surveys about, for example, the needs of a particular ethnic minority are of limited help in guiding purchasers unless seen in the context of equivalent surveys of other groups. Whether a policy directive is advocacy based or priority based depends on how it comes about. A set of recommendations based on lobbying will be much more prone to distorting resource use than one based on research. Arguably the Child B case moved from a priority setting to an advocacy framework when the debate moved from the health authority to the law courts.

5   **Is the needs assessment exploratory or definitive?** Some approaches to needs assessment are exploratory in that they highlight undefined or under-enumerated problems. This is particularly true of lifestyle surveys that estimate the size of risk groups such as alcohol abusers or teenage smokers. Surveys of the needs within specific client groups can also fall within this category but they differ from population surveys in that they often involve advocacy. If effectiveness of interventions has been determined prior to a population survey then this approach is compatible with epidemiological health care needs assessment.

6   **Is the determination of the most important needs expert or participatory?** The epidemiological approach to needs assessment is essentially an expert approach (with a population perspective). It seeks to be as objective as possible although no judgement of relative needs can be truly objective. Interpretation of data is partly subjective and the rules for decision making are inevitably value-laden. However the setting of priorities using an epidemiological and cost-effectiveness framework is markedly different from a process based on democratic consensus. Attempts to merge the two as in Oregon and in the local experience of many health authorities can have merit but the outcome will nearly always depend on the relative emphasis given to the provision of objective information and the extent to which participants can interpret them. As a general rule the expert approach to priority setting is more viable the further it is from the clinical decision making. At one extreme the World Health Organization's assessment of relative need operates by very clear cost-effectiveness rules.[29] At the other extreme the individual clinical decisions are rightly very open to patient views. District health authorities have to reconcile the two.

Underlying all of these questions is the further question: 'Who carries out the needs assessment and for what purpose?' Provided the assessment's aims and context are clearly stated and clearly understood there is a place for all of these approaches to needs assessment. Many can be subsumed within the approach used in this book in that they provide information about:

- numbers in a particular group, i.e. incidence and prevalence
- the effectiveness and cost-effectiveness of interventions
- the distribution of current services and their costs.

There is more information available on these elements of epidemiology-based needs assessment. Epidemiological studies contribute to the first point in the list above; effectiveness and outcomes research, i.e. evidence-based health care, to the second and assessments of current services to the third. The bringing together of the three themes in this book has been supported elsewhere at the extremes of individual and global needs assessments. For example Brewin's approach to measuring individual needs for mental health care identifies need as present when *both* function is impaired *and* when it is due to remedial cause.[30] Bobadilla *et al.*, in prescribing a minimum package for public health and clinical interventions for poor and middle income counties across all disease groups, identify both 'the size of the burden caused by a particular disease, injury and risk factor and the cost effectiveness of interventions to deal with it'.[29] Table 1 summarizes different approaches to health care needs assessment using the criteria discussed above.

Tools

In the first series of health care needs assessment we suggested three tools for needs assessment:

1 the epidemiological
2 comparative
3 corporate approaches.[2,3]

The definition of health care needs as the 'ability to benefit' implies an epidemiological approach. That is an assessment of how effective, for how many and, for the purposes of relative needs assessment, at what cost. However comparisons between localities (the comparative approach) and informed views of local service problems (the corporate approach) are important too.

The value of the 'comparative approach' is well demonstrated in the assessment of need for renal replacement therapy.[31] Increases in dialysis and transplantation in the UK closer to levels seen in better-provided European countries has been demonstrated over time to meet real needs. The need to change replacement levels from 20 per million in the 1960s, to 80 per million was suggested by both the comparative and epidemiological approach, i.e. of identifying incident end-stage renal failure and the effectiveness of renal replacement therapy. The comparative method does not however easily lead to cost-effectiveness considerations and is less successful in assessing which modality of renal replacement therapy is to be preferred; as the different balance between haemodialysis, peritoneal dialysis and transplantation rests on a variety of factors. The cost-effectiveness of different modalities is critical to priority setting. The comparative approach can however prompt key questions and therefore sets the priorities for more detailed analysis.

Almost every chapter of the first series of health care needs assessment expressed doubts about the extent and reliability of much of the routine data available for comparative analysis. The data on activity and prescribing, for example, would need to be linked to disease codes to represent faithfully true disease episodes. Disease registers such as those provided by the cancer registries can be invaluable and developments in information technology and unique patient numbers offer great scope for improved comparative analyses.

The 'corporate approach' involves the structured collection of the knowledge and views of informants on health care services and needs. Valuable information is often available from a wide range of parties, particularly including purchasing staff, provider clinical staff and general practitioners. Gillam points out that 'the intimate detailed knowledge of health professionals amassed over the years is often overlooked' and he particularly commends the insight of general practitioners, a suggestion well taken by many health authorities.[32] The corporate approach is essential if policies are to be sensitive to local circumstances. This approach might explore: first, a particularly prominent local need – such as the identification of severely mentally ill patients discharged from long-stay mental hospitals and lost to follow-up; second, consequences of local service considerations such as the balance between secondary and primary and local authority community care – as has been noted in the case of district nursing services;[33] third, where local needs differ from expectations based on national averages or typical expectations (due to local socioeconomic or environmental factors); and fourth, local popular concerns which may attach priorities to particular services

Table 1: Different approaches to health care needs assessment

Criterium	Health/social focus	Individual/population based	Resource/scarcity clear	Competing needs/advocacy	Definitive/exploratory	Expert/participatory
Population health care needs	Health	Population	Yes	Competing	Definitive	Expert
Individual health care needs	Health	Individual	Sometimes	Either	Definitive	Expert
Social services assessments	Social	Individual	Sometimes	Competing	Both	Both
Participatory planning	Social	Population	Sometimes	Competing	Definitive	Participatory
Oregon-style planning	Health	Population	Yes	Competing	Definitive	Both
Primary health care checks	Health	Individual	No	Competing	Exploratory	Expert
Primary health care case note audit	Health	Individual	No	Competing	Both	Expert
Population surveys	Health	Population	No	Competing	Exploratory	Expert
Client group surveys	Health	Population	No	Advocacy	Exploratory	Both
Specialty recommendations	Health	Population	No	Advocacy	Definitive	Expert
Effectiveness reviews	Health	Population	Yes	Competing	Definitive	Expert

or institutions (effectiveness considerations being equal). The need for cottage hospitals as opposed to large primary care units or other modes of community service provision might be an example. Clearly the potential pitfalls of informal corporate assessment of need are bias and vested interest that could cloud an objective view of the evidence. Nevertheless corporate memory should not be ignored.

The 'epidemiological approach' has been described fully.[3] It is worth reiterating that the epidemiological approach goes wider than epidemiology. It includes reviews of incidence and prevalence and also evidence about the effectiveness and relative cost-effectiveness of interventions, which, for service planners is increasingly seen as a focal concern. The epidemiological approach to needs assessment has helped pioneer what is now a sea-change towards evidence-based health care purchasing.

Evidence-based health care requires some rating of the quality of evidence. The first series required contributors to assess the strength of recommendation as shown in Table 2 adapted from the US Task Force on preventive health care.[34] This is now a mainstay of evidence-based medicine and it is retained in the present series.

Table 2: Analysis of service efficacy

Strength of recommendation	
A	There is good evidence to support the use of the procedure
B	There is fair evidence to support the use of the procedure
C	There is poor evidence to support the use of the procedure
D	There is fair evidence to reject the use of the procedure
E	There is good evidence to support the rejection of the use of the procedure

Quality of evidence	
(I)	Evidence obtained from at least one properly randomized controlled trial
(II-2)	Evidence obtained from well-designed cohort or case controlled analytic studies, preferably from more than one centre or research group
(II-3)	Evidence obtained from multiple timed series with or without the intervention, or from dramatic results in uncontrolled experiments
(III)	Opinions of respected authorities based on clinical experience, descriptive studies or reports of expert committees
(IV)[a]	Evidence inadequate owing to problems of methodology, e.g. sample size, length or comprehensiveness of follow-up, or conflict in evidence

Table adapted from US Task Force on Preventive Health Care.
[a]The final quality of evidence (IV) was introduced by Williams *et al.* for the surgical interventions considered in the first series.[35]

The changing background

Health care needs assessment was thrown into the spotlight in 1989 by the National Health Service Review.[36] The review, by separating purchasers and providers, identified population health care purchasing and therefore health care needs assessment as a distinct task. Since the beginning of the 1990s however a variety of circumstances has changed including the activities and research encompassed by health care needs assessment.

District health authority changes

The nature of the purchaser of health care at district health authority has changed in several ways. First, district mergers have resulted in larger purchasing units. Second the amalgamation of district health authorities with family health services authorities has extended the scope of purchasing and encouraged a more integrated approach to primary and secondary care services. Third the abolition of regional health authorities has necessitated careful purchasing of specialist services (these were formerly purchased regionally). Fourth the relationship between purchasers and providers of health care is showing some signs of maturing, as it has become obvious that large monopsonists (dominant purchasers) and monopolists have to work fairly closely together. Fifth there has been increased involvement of general practitioners (see below). These changes make districts potentially more sophisticated assessors of health care needs – although in practice such sophistication has been slowed by the administrative upheaval caused by the changes.

Cost containment

The second critical background circumstance affecting health care needs assessment is the increasing recognition of the need for cost containment. Although costs have always been constrained by the NHS allocation, new pressures have resulted from a variety of sources.

- Increased patient expectations – some of which have been encouraged centrally – particularly those concerning waiting times.
- New technologies with either a high unit cost, e.g. new drugs such as Beta Interferon for multiple sclerosis and DNase for cystic fibrosis, or which widen the indications for treatment, e.g. new joint replacement prostheses which have a longer life-span and can be given to younger patients.[37,38]
- New pressures at the boundaries between day health and social care in the problems of community care, and more recently with the criminal justice system – in the case of mentally disordered offenders.[39]

In theory the logic of needs assessment allows the identification of over-met need – in the sense of relatively ineffective and expensive services – as easily as undermet needs. In practice the former is more difficult to identify and much more difficult to correct. This further focuses attention on a limited number of areas and especially on a limited number of the most important cost pressures such as Beta Interferon.

General practitioner fundholding and GPs in purchasing

The third major background change has been the growing relative importance of general practice fundholding as a purchasing entity. In 1991 GP fundholding covered only around 10% of the population. One of the more striking aspects of the NHS reforms has been the expansion of fundholding which now (1996) covers more than half the population of England and Wales.[40] The scope of standard fundholding has been extended to cover the bulk of elective surgery outpatient care (except maternity and emergencies), community nursing and various direct access services. Some 70 total purchasing pilots have been established where GPs take on the entire NHS allocation for their patients. Side by side with these experiments in budget delegation is a variety of schemes whereby GPs are consulted, or otherwise involved in the commissioning of services.

Health care needs assessment in this book was designed primarily with district health authorities in mind. This reflected the dominant status of health authorities as purchasers at the time and also the size of the populations they covered. A population perspective makes more sense the larger the population, not least because the expected numbers of cases and their treatments are more predictable in larger populations. This is an issue for locality purchasing in general[41] and has even been a problem for district health authority purchasing when it comes to tertiary services and the rarer secondary services. The average GP sees only one case of thyroid cancer every 25 years and only eight heart attacks every year.[42] General practitioner fundholders cover populations ranging from 7000 to around 30 000. The total purchasing pilots which cover populations up to 80 000 only slightly ameliorate this. For GPs needs assessment as defined in this series is most likely to be applicable at the level of consortia with a large population. But taken together with GP involvement in profiling the population through case note audit and other means, needs assessment in primary care offers fruitful possibilities.

Evidence-based health care

The fourth main background change is in the drive from the research community itself. The evidence-based medicine and knowledge-based purchasing movement has been partly driven by imperatives to cost containment against a background of increasing health care costs as technology advances and by the acknowledgement that not all health care is effective[22,43] and by the differences in cost-effectiveness. The result is that needs assessment and cost-effectiveness assessment have become very closely related.

Use of the health care needs assessment series

Evidence for the usefulness of the epidemiological approach has come from the results of a survey of directors of public health in the UK[45], a Department of Health focus group on the first series, the House of Commons Health Committee's[46] review of the process by which authorities set priorities, and a national survey of contracting.[47] Two contrasting themes arising from these sources emerge.

1   There is an increasing appetite in health authorities for reliable material which assists priority setting. Health care purchasers are increasingly establishing a knowledge base across the whole range of health care, even if change is most effectively carried through by being reasonably selective.
2   Contracts themselves are not (yet) disease-based – usually built up from specialties they lack a starting point from which needs assessment can play a part. Thus although needs assessment has a role in setting the perspective for contracting, the guarantee that detailed implementation will take place is lacking. In part this reflects staffing shortages and the competing claims of other foci for purchasing (mergers, extra contractual referrals, waiting list initiatives, efficiency drives etc.). In part early attempts to develop disease-specific foci were hampered by poor quality data on patient treatment and particularly costs. This will become less of a problem not just with the growth of health technology assessment to provide the evidence base but also with initiatives such as the National Steering Group on Costing which has led to the costing of health care resource groups (HRGs) in six specialties.[48,49]

These surveys and experience with the first and second series have confirmed the usefulness of the protocol for health care needs assessment. Its six main elements remain:

1   a statement of the problem (normally a disease or intervention)
2   identifying the relevant sub-categories

3   the incidence and prevalence of the condition
4   the nature and level of service provided
5   the effectiveness (including the cost–effectiveness) of the service or treatments
6   models of care.

In addition authors have considered appropriate outcome measures, targets, the routine information available and current research priorities.

To extend the coverage and to link health care needs assessment more closely to the specialty basis of service planning this second series has moved away from single interventions and diseases to include groups of interventions (terminal and palliative care), groups of diseases/problems (sexually transmitted diseases, child and adolescent mental health) and whole specialties (gynaecology, dermatology and accident and emergency services) (Table 3). Only one review, on breast cancer, is defined as a disease group. Several of the reviews however use diseases as sub-categories. Back pain is defined more by the diagnostic cluster it represents than a disease group or aetiology.

Table 3: Health care needs assessment topics

	Series 1	Series 2
Cause	Alcohol misuse Drug abuse	
Diagnosis		Low back pain
Intervention	Total hip replacement Total knee replacement Cataract surgery Hernia repair Prostatectomy for benign prostatic hyperplasia Varicose vein treatments	
Group of interventions	Family planning, abortion and fertility services	Terminal and palliative care
Disease	Renal disease Diabetes mellitus Coronary heart disease Stroke (acute cerebrovascular disease) Colorectal cancer Dementia Cancer of the lung	Breast cancer
Heretogenous group of diseases/ problems	Lower respiratory disease Mental illness	Genitourinary medicine services Child and adolescent mental health
Service/specialty	Community child health services	Gynaecology Dermatology Accident and emergency departments
Client group	People with learning disabilities	

We believe that each of the authors of the eight reviews has admirably matched the task of reviewing the components of health care needs assessment of their disease topic. Furthermore the original protocol has stood up well in its first few years. This has been so against a turbulent background in health care purchasing and a background of only slow progress in the development and availability of health care information. At the same time epidemiologically-based needs assessment has been reinforced by its overlap with other initiatives towards effective health care as well as by its uniquely wide coverage of entire diseases, groups of interventions and specialties.

References

1 Stevens A, Gabbay J. Needs assessment, needs assessment. *Health Trends* 1991; **23**: 20–3.
2 National Health Service Management Executive. *Assessing Health Care Needs*. London: Department of Health, 1991.
3 Stevens A, Raftery J. Introduction. In *Health Care Needs Assessment, the epidemiologically based needs assessment reviews. Vol. 1*. Oxford: Radcliffe Medical Press, 1994.
4 Culyer A. *Need and the National Health Service*. London: Martin Robertson, 1976.
5 *House of Commons NHS and Community Care Act*. London: HMSO, 1990.
6 *Department of Health Care Programme Approach Guidelines*. London: Department of Health, 1990.
7 Gillam S, McCartney P, Thorogood M. Health promotion in primary care. *Br Med J* 1996; **312**: 324–5.
8 Harris A. Health checks for people over 75. *Br Med J* 1992; **305**: 599–600.
9 Whitkin B, Altschuld J. *Planning and conducting needs assessments. A practical guide*. California: Sage, 1995.
10 Oregon Health Services Commission. *Prioritisation of health services*: Salem: Oregon Health Commission, 1991.
11 National Health Service Management Executive. *Local voices*. London: Department of Health, 1992.
12 Mawhinney B. Speech at the National Purchasing Conference. 13 April 1994, Birmingham.
13 Ham C. Priority setting in the NHS: reports from six districts. *Br Med J* 1993; **307**: 435–8.
14 Price D. Lessons for health care rationing from the case of child B. *Br Med J* 1996; **312**: 167–9.
15 Murray S, Graham L. Practice based health need assessment: use of four methods in a small neighbourhood. *Br Med J* 1995; **310**: 1443–8.
16 Shanks J, Kheraj S, Fish S. Better ways of assessing health needs in primary care. *Br Med J* 1995; **310**: 480–1.
17 Jarman B. Underprivileged areas: validation and distribution scores. *Br Med J* 1984; **289**: 1587–92.
18 Gunnell D, Ewing S. Infertility, prevalence, needs assessment and purchasing. *J Public Health Med* 1994; **16**: 29–35.
19 Office of Population Censuses and Surveys. *General Household Survey*. London: HMSO, 1992.
20 Martin J, Meltzer H, Elliott D. *The prevalence of disability among adults*. London: HMSO, 1988.
21 Higginson I, Victor C. Needs assessment for older people. *J R Soc Med* 1994; **87**: 471–3.
22 Advisory Group on Health Technology Assessment. *Assessing the effects of health technologies, principles, practice, proposals*. London: Department of Health, 1993.
23 Standing Group on Health Technology. *Report of the NHS Health Technology Assessment Programme 1995*. London: Department of Health, 1995.
24 Courtney P, O'Grady J, Cunnane J. The provision of secure psychiatric services in Leeds; paper I, a point prevalence study. *Health Trends* 1992, **24**: 48–50.
25 Stevens A, Gooder P, Drey N. *The prevalence and needs of people with mental illness and challenging behaviour and the appropriateness of their care*. (In press.)
26 Wing J, Thornicroft G, Brewin C. Measuring and meeting mental health needs. In *Measuring mental health needs* (eds G Thornicroft, C Brewin, J Wing). London: Royal College of Psychiatrists, 1992.
27 Sheldon TA, Raffle A, Watt I. Why the report of the Advisory Group on osteoporosis undermines evidence based purchasing. *Br Med J* 1996; **312**: 296–7.
28 Royal College of Physicians. Care of elderly people with mental illness, specialist services and medical training. London: RCP, RCPsych., 1989.
29 Bobadilla J, Cowley P, Musgrove P *et al*. Design, content and finance of an essential national package of health services. In *Global comparative assessments in the health care sector* (eds C Murray, A Lopez). Geneva: World Health Organization, 1994.

30 Brewin C. Measuring individual needs of care and services. In *Measuring mental health needs* (eds G Thornicroft, C Brewin, J Wing). London: Royal College of Psychiatrists, 1997.

31 Beech R, Gulliford M, Mays N *et al.* Renal disease. In *Health Care Needs Assessment, the epidemiologically based needs assessment reviews. Vol. 1.* Oxford: Radcliffe Medical Press, 1994.

32 Gillam S. Assessing the health care needs of populations – the general practitioners' contribution. *Brit J General Practice* 1992; **42**: 404–5.

33 Conway M, Armstrong D, Bickler G. A corporate needs assessment for the purchase of district nursing: a qualitative approach. *Public Hlth* 1995; **109**: 3337–45.

34 US Preventive Services Task Force. *Guide to clinical preventive services. An assessment of the effectiveness of 169 interventions.* Baltimore: Williams and Wilkins, 1989.

35 Williams M H, Frankel S J, Nanchahal K *et al.* Total hip replacements. In *Health Care Needs Assessment, the epidemiologically based needs assessment reviews. Vol. I.* Oxford: Radcliffe Medical Press, 1994.

36 Department of Health. *Working for patients.* London: HMSO, 1989.

37 Stevens A (ed.). Health technology evaluation research reviews. *Wessex Institute of Public Health Medicine. Vol. 2,* 1994 (248 pp) and *Vol. 3,* 1995 (285 pp).

38 Raftery J, Couper N, Stevens A. *Expenditure implications of new technologies in the NHS – an examination of 20 technologies.* Southampton: WIPHM, 1996.

39 Department of Health, Home Office. *Review of health and social services for mentally disordered offenders and others requiring similar services: final summary report.* London: HMSO, 1992. (The Reed Committee report).

40 Audit Commission. *What the doctor ordered. A study of GP fundholders in England Wales.* London: HMSO, 1996.

41 Ovretveit J. *Purchasing for health.* Buckingham: Oxford University Press, 1995.

42 Fry J. *General practice: the facts.* Oxford: Radcliffe Medical Press, 1993.

43 Chalmers I, Enkin M, Keirse M (eds). *Effective care in pregnancy and childbirth.* Oxford: Oxford University Press, 1989.

44 Neuburger H. *Cost-effectiveness register: user guide.* London: Department of Health, 1992.

45 Stevens A. *Epidemiologically based needs assessment series evaluation results.* 1993, unpublished.

46 House of Commons Health Committee. *Priority setting in the NHS: purchasing.* Minutes of evidence and appendices. London: HMSO, 1994.

47 *Purchasing Unit Review of Contracting – the third national review of contracting 1994–5.* Leeds: National Health Service Executive, 1994.

48 *Costing for contracting FDL(93)59.* Leeds: National Health Service Executive, 1993.

49 *Comparative cost data: the use of costed HRGs to inform the contracting process. EL(94)51.* Leeds: National Health Service Executive, 1994.

Palliative and Terminal Care

I Higginson

1 Summary

This chapter provides assistance for those purchasing palliative care services. The analysis is based on current research evidence and national and local population and health services utilization data.

- Palliative care is the active total care of patients whose disease is not responsive to curative treatment. Control of pain, of other symptoms, and of psychological, social and spiritual problems is paramount. The goal of palliative care is achievement of the best possible quality of life for patients and their families.
- Modern approaches to palliative care have evolved since the 1960s. Hospices, domiciliary and home palliative care teams have evolved rapidly, to provide specialist palliative care, particularly for patients with advanced cancer.
- General palliative care approaches and attitudes such as good pain control and holistic care are needed by all health care professionals caring for people with advanced disease, particularly when curative measures are unhelpful or inappropriate. The specialist palliative care services such as hospices and home care teams are immediately concerned with only one segment of care.
- Funding arrangements between the NHS and specialist palliative care services vary. 75% of hospices are voluntary or charitable units, although many have contracts with health authorities.
- National and local data on the incidence and prevalence can be used to calculate the likely numbers of patients and families needing palliative care. The absolute numbers of patients dying from cancer and other diseases likely to have a palliative period are available from OPCS records. Applying the prevalence of symptoms to this population gives estimates of the range of problems and the size of population needing care.

  Within a population of 1 000 000 there are approximately 2800 cancer deaths per year and of these 2400 people will experience pain, 1300 will have trouble with breathing and 1400 will have symptoms of vomiting or nausea in their last year of life. There will be approximately 6900 deaths, due to progressive non-malignant disease and some of these will have had a period of advancing progressive disease when palliative care would have been appropriate. 4600 people will have suffered pain, 3400 will have had trouble with breathing and 1900 will have had symptoms of vomiting or nausea in the last year of life.
- A wide range of services is available. These include specialist palliative care services, such as hospices and mobile palliative care teams and general services, including primary and hospital care. Voluntary organizations, support groups and local authority services also play a significant role.
- Studies of the effectiveness of care have tended to demonstrate weaknesses in conventional care alone and support the use of inpatient hospices and mobile support teams, especially those operating in the community. Cost-effectiveness studies suggest that these services are not more expensive than conventional care and in some instances may be cheaper.

  However these evaluations have usually been confined to cancer patients and have been based on services where only a proportion of eligible patients and families received care. Therefore the proportion of patients that should most cost-effectively receive specialist care is not known. Furthermore services vary in their structure and methods of working, although a multi-professional approach appears to be that most recommended, further comparisons are needed to identify the most cost-effective models of specialist service provision.

- Evaluations of day care, hospice at home and services for children are limited and further work is needed in these areas.
- Examples of models of care for health districts, outcome measures, targets and service specifications are given. Many of the measures and service specifications are being tested in populations and services.
- The chapter concludes with recommendations for future research, including evaluation of those services currently unevaluated, cost-effectiveness studies and comparison of outcome measures, and recommendations for information, including the agreement of standard data sets based on those currently being piloted by various organizations.

2 Introduction

This chapter assists purchasing authorities in developing their needs assessments and setting service specifications for palliative care.

Development of palliative care

Uncontrolled symptoms or severe patient and family distress while a patient has a progressive illness severely inhibits the patient's quality of life and is believed to impact on the carers' or family members' subsequent resolution of their grief.[1,2] Palliative care seeks to control the symptoms and support the patient and family.[2,3] It aims to improve the quality of life and therefore offers health gain, in terms of adding health and life to years rather than extending life expectancy, for patients and their family members and carers. Death is an inevitable companion of life and therefore the appropriate care for people who are dying is a concern for all health districts. Changes in the nature of diseases during this last century have led to many more people dying from chronic diseases in later life rather than suddenly from acute infection.[2] Patients are increasingly likely to experience a palliative period during their illness.[2]

Modern approaches to palliative care are usually thought to have commenced in the 1950s and 60s with the development of the hospice movement. Dame Cicely Saunders worked in early hospices and in 1967 founded St Christopher's Hospice in Sydenham.[4] The Marie Curie Foundation was created in 1948 and, following a survey of 7000 cancer patients in their own homes in 1952, established a programme of a day and night home nursing service and nursing homes.[5] These developments were strongly supported by research evidence based on the reports of bereaved relatives or occasionally from patients. This indicated that existing care for patients with advanced disease, whether in hospital or at home, failed to meet patients' needs for pain and symptom control, psychosocial care, spiritual care, communication and information and care for the family.[2,4] Although many patients with advanced disease continued to be cared for by conventional health and social services, specialist palliative care services developed either to directly provide care or to provide education and support for the existing services.

During the 1970s, inpatient hospices were the principal type of specialist palliative services to be developed. Many of these operated from voluntary or charity run units, although some were created within the NHS. They concentrated on care for cancer patients and some, mainly the larger hospices, developed educational programmes for doctors, nurses and other health and social professionals. These programmes recognized that a great many patients were cared for by their primary care team in the community or by hospital staff, and sought to educate and support those working in these settings, providing updates in the most recent methods of symptom control and patient and family care.[2-6]

Although the number of inpatient hospices continued to grow, more and more emphasis was placed on the development of home care teams working from hospices and multi-professional palliative care teams in hospitals or the community. In 1980 a working group on terminal care advised that efforts should concentrate on educating and training hospital and community staff and supporting them in their work.[1] It was suggested that support teams, either in the hospital or community, could fulfil this need. The advice of the working group was partly ignored – hospices continued to grow as quickly as support teams – but support teams began to rapidly increase in numbers.[2] Recently the number of support teams has overtaken the number of inpatient hospices.

Support teams comprised specialist staff who would offer advice and support to health workers in the community or in hospitals. Teams were usually centred specifically on trained nurses (often initially funded by the Cancer Relief Macmillan Fund with an agreement that the health authority or Trust would take over funding after three to five years and called Macmillan nurses). Medical, social work and sometimes other professional support were usually provided, and in larger teams doctors, social workers and occasionally physiotherapists or occupational therapists were members of the team. Some teams worked specifically in the hospital while others worked exclusively in the community and in some instances the team would carry out both roles. Teams usually worked within geographically defined areas and did not take over from existing hospital or community nurses, or provide hands-on care.[2-7]

The most recent developments of specialist services have been in the areas of:

- **Day care** This can be operated by an inpatient hospice or a palliative care team.[2,3]
- **Hospice at home** Builds on existing community services and support teams but can also provide 24-hour nursing or sitting care at home, in a similar way to or by collaboration with Marie Curie day and night home nurses.
- **Specialist outpatient clinics** May be medical, or for lymphoedema or for families requiring intensive social work input.

These services encompass the hospice or palliative care philosophy (see the definitions of palliative care on page 5 and in Appendix II).

Philosophies of palliative care: home, hospital, hospice

Different philosophies regarding the most appropriate mix of services and the balance between home and institutional care have developed. Cartwright demonstrated, from random samples of deaths in England, that the proportions of patients who died in institutions increased between 1969 and 1987 from 46% to 50% (hospitals) and 5% to 18% (hospices and other institutions), while the proportion who died at home reduced from 42% to 24%.[8] In 1993 in England and Wales, 23% of all deaths and 26% of cancer deaths occurred at home.[9] Bowling argued against the 'institutionalisation' of death on the grounds that home death was more natural and that a person would have more chance to influence their quality of life.[10]

The development of domiciliary palliative care teams, home nursing services and, more recently, hospice at home and day care, sought to reverse this shift towards institutional care, by increasing the support for patients, their families and other community services. But hospitals, hospices and the increasing role of residential and nursing homes cannot be overlooked – because the majority of patients are cared for in these settings for at least part of their illness. Thus in many areas a wide range of palliative services has developed to attempt to meet needs and to provide choice. Development was often piecemeal and followed varying inputs, including planned need, response to inadequacies, local interest, active voluntary groups, concern within the NHS and champions of a particular approach.[2] However in 1987 a Department of Health circular required health authorities to examine their arrangements for terminal care;[11] this was followed by some funding.[12–16]

Funding arrangements

Financial relationships between palliative services and the NHS vary. The voluntary sector was responsible for the development of many of the specialist palliative care services, particularly inpatient hospices. Usually local groups who were committed to the idea were responsible for raising funds and establishing the hospice. During the 1970s and 1980s only a few of the inpatient hospices were funded or developed entirely by the NHS. In 1995 a large proportion (75%) of hospice inpatient care was provided by voluntary or independent hospice units. These are registered charities most of which have firm links in policy and practice with the NHS from whom they receive varying amounts of funding to supplement funds raised in their local community.[17] Three national charities are also involved in the provision of inpatient care: Marie Curie Cancer Care, the Cancer Relief Macmillan Fund and the Sue Ryder Foundation. Other charities also provide funding for hospices or specialist palliative care services, such as Help the Hospices.

In 1988 the Department of Health began to allocate money, top sliced from the NHS budget and distributed by regional health authorities, specifically for voluntary hospices and specialist palliative care services.[12] During the early 1990s the allocation rose rapidly – from £8 million in 1989 to £17 million in 1991 and £37 million in 1992.[2,13,14] In 1994/95 funding was: £35.7 million for specialist palliative care services (the regional allocations are shown in Appendix I), £5.7 million DSS transfer for voluntary hospices and £6.3 million for drugs for voluntary hospices.[15] This was built into recurrent baselines for health authorities and ceased to be separately identified from 1995/96.[16] Health authorities were encouraged to enter into three-year contracts. Other inpatient care was already funded and managed by the NHS in designated wards specifically for palliative care.[17]

The NHS was more active in the development of home and hospital support teams and was either responsible for the development of many services or took over funding from the Cancer Relief Macmillan Fund after an initial period of 3–5 years of funding. EL(94)14 stated that many authorities already fund NHS specialist palliative provision and that these existing levels of support, wherever possible, should be maintained. The separately identified funding was not intended to be used to take over the funding of nursing services provided within the three year pump priming from the Cancer Relief Macmillan Fund and the NHS contribution already committed to Marie Curie Cancer Care Nursing Services.[15] Many independent or voluntary hospices also provide home care teams and day care services.[17]

Key issues

Appropriate care for people with advanced disease is generally a high priority among patients and consumers. This is evidenced by the development of hospices within the voluntary sector. After public consultation in the Oregon Priority Setting exercise in the US, 'comfort care', such as palliative treatment, was ranked the seventh highest priority (and in some versions, the fifth) out of 17 categories of care.[18] In the UK health districts have also found that palliative care or care for people who were dying came usually in the top 8–15 priorities, depending on the descriptors used.[19,20]

Despite the development of specialist palliative services, it is widely recognized that most patients who have progressive illness which is no longer curable (see page 5) receive much of their care from the primary care team and hospital staff. Specialist palliative care services have tended to concentrate on offering a service for cancer patients. They also receive those patients who have the most severe symptoms or for whom family distress is most severe.[2,4] However a recent joint report of the Standing Medical Advisory Committee and Standing Nursing Advisory Committee included among its recommendations that:

- all patients needing them should have access to palliative care services
- similar services should be developed for patients dying from diseases other than cancer.[4]

Health districts were encouraged to determine levels of need among all patients and to purchase an appropriate mix of services, including the specialist palliative care services. However this leaves health districts to determine what mix of services should be purchased to provide the most cost-effective and high quality care for their local population. Health commissioners also have to decide what constitutes a specialist palliative care service. These services vary in their levels of trained staff and there has been recent concern that some nursing homes or units without staff trained in palliative care will rename themselves as specialist services without being able to offer this type of specialized care. This chapter aims to provide assistance in the needs assessment for palliative and terminal care and follows the format proposed by Stevens and Raftery.[21]

3 Statement of the problem

Definitions of palliative care, terminal care and the specialist services

This section sets out the main definitions and terms relevant to this field.

Palliative care

There are various definitions of palliative care. The most straightforward is that of the National Council for Hospice and Specialist Palliative Care Services, which is based on an earlier definition from the World Health Organization:[22-24]

Palliative care is the active total care of patients whose disease is not responsive to curative treatment. Control of pain, of other symptoms and of psychological, social and spiritual problems is paramount. The goal of palliative care is achievement of the best possible quality of life for patients and their families. Many aspects of palliative care are also applicable earlier in the course of the illness, in conjunction with anticancer treatment. Palliative care:

- affirms life and regards dying as a normal process
- neither hastens nor postpones death
- provides relief from pain and other distressing symptoms
- integrates the psychological and spiritual aspects of patient care
- offers a support system to help patients live as actively as possible until death
- offers a support system to help the family cope during the patient's illness and in their own bereavement.

A similar definition is from the Standing Medical Advisory Committee and Standing Nursing and Midwifery Advisory Committee (1992):[4]

Palliative care is active total care offered to a patient with a progressive illness and their family when it is recognised that the illness is no longer curable, in order to concentrate on the quality of life and the alleviation of distressing symptoms within the framework of a co-ordinated service. Palliative care neither hastens nor postpones death; it provides a relief from pain and other distressing symptoms and integrates the psychological and spiritual aspects of care. In addition it offers a support system to help during the patient's illness and in bereavement. 'Family' is used as a general term to cover closely-attached individuals, whatever their legal status.

A key feature of this second definition is that the disease is described as 'progressive'. It distinguishes between chronic diseases which may not be curable but are unchanging – such as patients with unchanging diabetes – and those diseases that are progressive and likely to result in a patient dying – such as advanced lung cancer. For this reason and because of its comprehensiveness, it is the SMAC/SNMAC definition above which will be used in this chapter.

Other definitions include the above but tend to expand or elaborate on some of the aspects of care offered. Common other definitions include:

From the European Association for Palliative Care:[25]

Palliative care is care for the dying by providing active, total care at a time when disease is not responsive to curative treatment. Control of pain, of other symptoms and of psychological, social and spiritual problems is paramount. The goal of care for the dying is the highest possible quality of life for the patient and family.

Terminal illness and terminal care

Terminal illness refers to active and progressive disease for which curative treatment is neither possible nor appropriate and from which death is certain. This varies from a few days to many months.[4]

For the purpose of the DSS income support limits for people suffering from a terminal illness and within NHS executive letters a definition that 'terminally ill people are those with active and progressive disease for which curative treatment is not possible or not appropriate and from which death can reasonably be expected within 12 months' is adopted.[16,26]

Terminal care is an important part of palliative care and usually refers to the management of patients during their last few days or weeks or even months of life from a point at which it becomes clear that the patient is in a progressive state of decline.

Palliative medicine

Palliative medicine has been recognized as a specialty in its own right.[4] Postgraduate training is available for doctors intending to practise in this specialty in centres approved by the Joint Committee for Higher Medical Training and for general practitioners (GPs) during after-vocational training. Academic, medical and nursing posts have been created.[4]

When palliative medicine became a specialty the Association of Palliative Medicine provided the definition:

Palliative medicine is the appropriate medical care of patients with advanced and progressive disease for whom the focus of care is the quality of life and in whom the prognosis is limited (though sometimes may be several years). Palliative medicine includes consideration of the family's needs before and after the patient's death.[24]

Note that this definition refers to 'medicine' and thereby the activities of doctors. Clinical nurse specialists in palliative care must also complete post-registration training in palliative care.

Sub-categories of services: definitions of specialist care services

The principles and practices of palliative care are not the exclusive concern of the specialist services.[24] The relief of suffering is the general responsibility of doctors, nurses and other health care professionals over the whole continuum of diagnosis to death. General palliative care approaches and attitudes should be part of normal clinical practice.[24]

Specialist palliative care services are immediately concerned with only one segment of that spectrum of care. They are committed to controlling pain and other symptoms, easing suffering and sustaining the last phase of life in patients who have active, progressive and far advanced disease which is no longer amenable to curative treatment. Their work integrates the physical, psychological, social and spiritual aspects of care enabling dying patients to live with dignity and offering support to them, their families and carers during the patient's illness and their bereavement. All patients with progressive disease would benefit from a palliative approach and a smaller group need specialist care.

The following section outlines the main terms. Further information is given in Appendix II.

Hospice

The term hospice is used in two ways. The first refers to the philosophy of hospice care, which is in effect the same as the philosophy and principles of palliative care in the definitions above.[22] The second refers to a hospice unit. Usually this is a free standing unit with inpatient facilities, which practises palliative care emphasizing medical and psychosocial care. It will normally have medical and nursing staff specially trained in palliative care and the control of symptoms and has a high nurse to patient ratio. Hospices will usually offer symptom control and terminal, palliative and respite care. Many hospices also offer day care and home support teams. Some hospices do not offer inpatient care. To avoid confusion this chapter refers to the types of facilities offered by the hospice – e.g. inpatient care etc. Note also that there is a wide variety of types and grades of staff operating within different hospices. This is discussed in section 6.

Funding for hospices may be charitable, from the local community or national charities, or from the NHS, or a combination of these.[2] There is debate about what levels of staffing constitute an inpatient specialist service (Appendix II).[22]

Specialist palliative care teams

These teams are found in three main categories.

1 Hospital palliative care teams

These teams aim to bring the principles and benefits of palliative care into acute hospitals. The teams usually work in an advisory capacity providing symptom control and psychological support to patients and carers as well as playing an important role in education and advice within the hospital. Most teams are made up of two or more clinical nurse specialists and many are multi-disciplinary, including a doctor, social worker, chaplain and others.[2,4,22]

2 Domiciliary or home palliative care teams

These teams comprise specialist staff who offer advice and support to health workers in the community. It is usually centred on clinical nurse specialists (often Macmillan nurses) with medical and other professional support and the team may be attached to a general hospital with a cancer unit, inpatient hospice/palliative care unit or the community nursing service. The team does not take over responsibility from the community nurse or GP and does not usually deliver bedside nursing care.[2,4,22]

3 Palliative care teams

These teams combine elements of the hospital and domiciliary element, either with some team staff working in the community and others in the hospital or with staff working with individual patients and following them from setting to setting.[2,4,22,27]

Marie Curie nurses

These nurses offer a day and night nursing and sitting service, which complements the community nursing service.[4,5]

Multi-disciplinary care

This is the team approach to palliative care, which recognizes that many health care workers have roles to play. Each patient's key worker may vary according to the particular problem of the patient and local factors.

Day care

This is provided by a growing number of palliative care units and other facilities to enable patients to continue living at home. Day care is particularly valuable for patients who need more than outpatient and GP services and where carers need support. It also serves to introduce patients to a service without admission to inpatient care.[4,22]

Rehabilitation

In the context of palliative care, rehabilitation refers to assisting patients to achieve and maintain their maximum physical, emotional, spiritual, vocational and social potential, however limited this may be as a result of the progression of disease.[4]

If rehabilitation is effective and efficient, it may be of particular value to patients who are not terminal in enabling them to return home and obtain an improved quality of life.

Further descriptions of these services and terms are shown in Appendix II and in the definitions published by the National Council for Hospice and Specialist Palliative Care Services.[22] A national directory of services can be obtained from St Christopher's Hospice Information Service (see Appendix II).

Sub-categories of diseases and types of patient who need palliative care

This epidemiologically based needs assessment is very different from the previous disease based reviews and is more similar to the epidemiological reviews of a client group, such as the assessment for elderly people. As the earlier definitions suggest, palliative care encompasses patients who suffer from different diseases, with different rates of progression. Patients who need palliative care are not a homogenous group, although they are similar in having active, progressive disease where the emphasis needs to be on quality of life for the patient and their family.

Patients who have palliative needs can be grouped in several ways: by diagnosis, by symptoms or problems experienced or by type of care received. The first two of these would relate to the epidemiology of diseases and problems and thus are more useful in an assessment of need. The primary diagnosis can indicate whether a patient is likely to experience a palliative period, and whether they would develop problems and symptoms which would need a palliative approach or to be referred to a specialist palliative service. Data on the prevalence and incidence of diseases are available and can be obtained from mortality statistics. Some data on the likely incidence and prevalence of symptoms are available but much less is known about the incidence and prevalence of other problems – such as psychosocial, emotional or spiritual problems – experienced by patients, their families or carers.

The type of care received is affected by the availability of services across the country. This varies widely and so this indicator is less useful to assess need.

This chapter uses all of these three sub-categories but concentrates more on the first two.

The main primary diseases which can have a palliative period – i.e. a period when the disease is progressive, no longer curable and where the emphasis is the quality of life follow.

Types of illness

- Cancer, main categories are of:
  a) lung, trachea, bronchus
  b) ear, nose and throat
  c) female breast
  d) lymphatic
  e) digestive tract
  f) genitourinary
  g) leukaemia
  h) haemopoietic.
- Progressive non-malignant diseases, which can have a palliative period. These include:
  a) diseases of the circulatory system e.g. cardiovascular, cerebro–vascular diseases
  b) diseases of the respiratory system
  c) diseases of the nervous system and sense organs e.g. motor neurone disease, multiple sclerosis, dementia
  d) AIDS/HIV
- Children's terminal illnesses and hereditary diseases, including:
  a) hereditary degenerative disorder e.g. muscular dystrophy
  b) cystic fibrosis.

To estimate the need among these populations we have estimated the numbers of patients who may experience the different symptoms encountered – e.g. pain, dyspnoea etc. Such symptoms and problems would require treatment, often involving a palliative approach. Alternative estimates have also been based on the current use of services.

4 Prevalence and incidence

Current situation

The incidence of patients needing palliative care (either the general approach and/or specialist input) can be estimated from death rates of common conditions[9,28] which may require palliative care (Table 1).

Table 1: Death rates per million population by age group for common conditions in England (1993)

Age (years)	Sex	Neoplasms	Diseases of the circulatory system	Diseases of the respiratory system	Diseases of the nervous system and sense organs
All ages	M	3017	4830	1174	222
	F	2648	5016	1175	228
1–4	M	41	14	27	40
	F	37	10	18	37
5–14	M	40	7	5	18
	F	29	6	4	16
15–24	M	63	29	15	42
	F	50	22	12	21
25–34	M	120	83	34	42
	F	142	46	13	27
35–44	M	388	443	70	66
	F	547	149	34	44
45–54	M	1402	1707	168	89
	F	1586	506	111	77
55–64	M	4864	6109	772	188
	F	3941	2356	518	153
65–74	M	12621	17517	3376	567
	F	7668	9034	1876	404
75–84	M	23532	43559	11575	1985
	F	12404	29517	5492	1187
85 and over	M	34529	88641	37272	4323
	F	16868	76305	22709	2752

Widening the definition of patients who may need palliative care beyond those with cancers could triple the number of people included. Only some people with these conditions would require specialist palliative care. Each disease would have roughly three groups of patients:

- those who have a palliative period of advancing, progressive disease
- those who have stable or no disease, relatively few symptoms but then deteriorate or die suddenly (e.g. from a myocardial infarct)
- those who suffer from chronic disease, where the disease is not clearly progressing, but who might have periods of progression and symptoms where they would benefit from palliative care and then periods of remission.

In cancer patients the period of progression is most clearly predicted and many would fall into the first category. However the other conditions, such as circulatory disease, may often fall into the other two categories. There is little research into the natural history of these diseases as death approaches and we do not know what proportion of patients experience a period of advancing disease suitable for specialist palliative treatment, although all would probably benefit from palliative approaches and principles. However symptoms experienced in the last year of life can provide us with some information about whether the patient was disease free or had symptoms which may be suited to palliative treatment. The likely symptoms in these groups for individual diseases are estimated below.

Calculating numbers of deaths in the population

This population needs assessment is based on a population of 1 000 000.

It is assumed that the population includes people from a range of different cultural and ethnic groups. It is also assumed that there is a range of health experiences across the different wards or localities within an area, with the most disadvantaged wards displaying higher rates of death and increased levels of illness, high levels of unemployment and poorer housing, with many single parent families and elderly people who live alone.

Mortality statistics provide details of the numbers of deaths occurring in the population, totally and for different causes. Within a population of 1 000 000 we would expect about 11 000 deaths per year.[28] Actual numbers for the population can be obtained from OPCS records. Anonymous records of the death registrations are made available to health authorities from OPCS via NHS executive regional health authorities, each year. Although a breakdown of the numbers and main causes of death are provided the raw data can be also obtained in a format suitable for local analysis in a spreadsheet or in a statistical package. For a small charge OPCS will also undertake specified analysis for individual populations if this is not possible locally. Some health authorities themselves collected and computerized data from the copies of death registrations which were automatically copied to them.

A breakdown of the likely data on deaths is shown in Table 2 and Figure 1. If the population follows the general pattern of England,[9,28] cancer would account for 25% of all deaths (27% for deaths in men and 23% for deaths in women). Cancers of the gastro-intestinal tract, trachea, bronchus and lung, and breast would be the most common (Table 2 and Figure 2). Circulatory disease would be the most common cause of death (45% men, 46% women). Respiratory disease would probably be the next most common after cancer (11% in men and in women).

Data from the public health common data set will provide the standardized mortality ratios (SMRs). These can be calculated for different causes of death and can be used to show whether cancers or other causes of mortality are more, less or equally common in the population compared with England and Wales. The SMR can also be calculated for different localities within the population, to show whether any of these vary in different ways. An example of the SMRs for one population is shown in Appendix III. Because the area shown appears to have an excess of cancer deaths, this may mean that higher than average palliative services are needed. However more accurate estimates of need for services are available by calculating the numbers of people who may have required palliative care locally and the prevalence of symptoms.

Cancer patients who may have required palliative care

The number of cancer patients with advanced disease and symptoms can be estimated from the number of cancer deaths. Some patients may have a short or not identified terminal period but the majority would have a clear period where they would require palliative care. The World Health Organization has recommended that for cancer patients the palliative approach should be a gradually increasing component of care from diagnosis onwards, rather than being confined to the last few weeks of life. This concept is shared by the

Table 2: Number of deaths in the population during one year for the most common causes (total population 1 million)

Cause of death	Men	Women	Total
Neoplasms[a]	1464	1341	2805
Circulatory system	2429	2624	5053
Respiratory system	595	626	1221
Chronic liver and cirrhosis	34	26	60
Nervous system and sense organs[b]	88	88	176
Senile and pre-senile organic conditions	22	22	44
Endocrine, nutritional, metabolic, immunity	187	123	310
Total of these diseases	4819	4850	9669
Total deaths from all causes[c]	5356	5644	11000

Cause of death			
Neoplasms include:			
Lip, oral, pharynx, larynx	41	34	75
Digestive and peritoneum	449	339	788
Trachea, bronchus, lung	394	291	685
Female breast	0	255	255
Genitourinary	243	178	421
Lymphatic and haemopoietic	154	54	208
Other, unspecified	7	7	14
Nervous system and sense organs include:			
Parkinson's disease	37	28	65
Multiple sclerosis	1	1	2
Meningitis	4	4	8

[a,b] For a breakdown of main groups see lower half of table.
[c] Deaths in those aged under 28 days excluded.

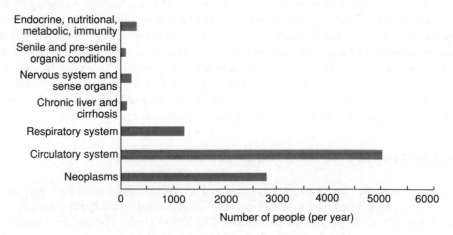

Figure 1: Main causes of death in the district: excluding those aged below 28 days.

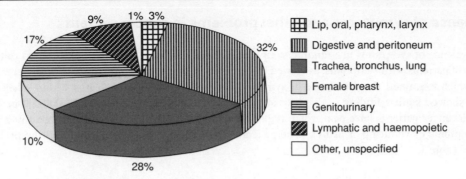

Figure 2: Main cancers in the district.

Expert Advisory Group on Cancer in their report on commissioning cancer services.[29] Implementation of this report's recommendations is underway.[30]

The data from Table 1 suggest that there may be 2800 people who die from cancer each year within a population of 1 000 000. Estimates of the proportions of these with symptoms should suggest the numbers who would benefit from palliative care advice, the palliative approach and, in some cases, specialist services such as hospice or home care.

Estimating the prevalence of symptoms and other problems in cancer and in patients with progressive non-malignant diseases

Studies which estimate the prevalence of symptoms among patients with cancer have been confined to selected populations, such as patients attending oncology clinics or patients admitted to a hospice service. Prospective data on the prevalence of symptoms and problems among patients with advancing non-malignant disease are rare and usually confined to those few patients referred to a palliative service. There is no prospective data on the prevalence of problems among patients not referred to these services, and such data are needed for an epidemiologically based needs assessment.

However one method of overcoming this sample bias is to identify patients after their death using the death registration. This approach has two drawbacks. First death registrations include inaccuracies – for example the recording of diagnosis is unreliable especially in elderly patients.[31] Second assessment of problems is made by the bereaved carers or spouse rather than the patient. Studies have suggested that spouses or carers may unreliably record some symptoms and anxieties when compared to patients' assessments.[32,33] On average carers or spouses tended to record slightly more severe problems than did the patients.[33] Psychological symptoms may be less accurately recorded.[34] Assessments made during bereavement appear to concord less than those made prospectively.[35] It may be that the carers' assessment is altered by their own grief and anxieties. Furthermore for some aspects of care, e.g. anxiety, the carers' and staff assessments agreed and recorded problems, whereas patients' ratings did not. Until prospective data on the prevalence of symptoms in complete populations of patients with advanced disease become available, these estimates based on the retrospective views of carers are needed. They at least provide the carers' views of whether patients need help for these symptoms. Given that the carer is part of the unit of palliative care, their view has some validity.

Prevalence of symptoms and other problems in cancer patients

The prevalence of symptoms in a random sample of national deaths in 1987 has been used to calculate the numbers of patients with symptoms, as viewed by bereaved carers, in the population.[8,36] A more recent study (1991) which examined the prevalence of symptoms in random samples of deaths within selected health districts showed similar findings.[37–40] These suggest that, among the population of 1 000 000 people, each year 2400 cancer patients have pain which requires treatment, 1300 have trouble with breathing and 1400 have symptoms of vomiting or nausea. The patients usually have several symptoms and the prevalence is shown in Table 3.

Table 3: Cancer patients: prevalence of problems (per 1 000 000 population)

Symptom	% with symptom in last year of life[a]	Estimated number in each year
Pain	84	2357
Trouble with breathing	47	1318
Vomiting or nausea	51	1431
Sleeplessness	51	1431
Mental confusion	33	926
Depression	38	1065
Loss of appetite	71	1992
Constipation	47	1318
Bedsores	28	785
Loss of bladder control	37	1038
Loss of bowel control	25	701
Unpleasant smell	19	533
Total deaths from cancer		**2805**

[a] As per Cartwright and Seale study,[8,36] based on a random sample of deaths and using the reports of bereaved carers.
Note: Patients usually have several symptoms.

Patients with cancer are known to have a higher prevalence of anxiety and depression when compared to the normal population. Anxiety and depression are often under-diagnosed.[31,41] High patient anxiety and family distress and anxiety are known to be associated with multiple symptoms, distressing or socially unacceptable symptoms (e.g. unpleasant smell) and poor symptom control.[3]

There are no population-based epidemiological studies which describe the levels of anxiety among patients and their families in the general cancer population. However studies based on referrals to palliative care teams have suggested that approximately one-third of families and one-quarter of patients describe severe anxiety, fears or worries.[34,42–44] This would translate into approximately 930 family members or family groups and 700 patients per 1 000 000 population. These people would need more intensive support and some would require specialist services.

Estimates based on use of specialist care services in cancer patients

Studies have suggested that in the UK between 15 and 25% of cancer deaths received inpatient hospice care and between 25 and 65% of cancer deaths received input from a support team or Macmillan nurse.[8,36-38,42,43,45,46] Applying these figures to the population would suggest that 700–1800 cancer patients require support team care and 400–700 should require inpatient hospice care (Table 4). Some patients will require both services and some patients would be admitted to hospice care two or more times.

Table 4: Cancer patients: need for specialist palliative services based on national and regional estimates of use (per 1 000 000 population)[a]

	Number of adults	%
Deaths from cancer in one year	2805	
Needing support team	701–1824	25–65
Needing inpatient hospice care	421–701	15–25

[a] Studies used include: Bennett and Corcoran (1994);[42] Cartwright (1991);[8] Seale (1991);[36] Higginson, Wade, McCarthy (1992);[43] Addington-Hall (1991);[37-40] Frankel (1990);[46] Eve and Jackson (1994).[45]

Given the fairly high prevalence of symptoms in cancer, it is likely that this figure is a conservative estimate. Furthermore national studies of the needs of cancer patients, given current provision, have demonstrated unmet needs for patients in terms of home support, symptom control and respite care.[8,36-38] As outlined on page 184 services have often developed in a piecemeal fashion; this limits the value of estimates based on current national use.

Patients with progressive non-malignant diseases who may have required palliative care

The numbers of patients with other causes of advanced disease and symptoms can be estimated from the numbers of non-cancer deaths within the health authority. Patients may have short or no identified terminal periods, some will die suddenly, but many who die from circulatory disorders, respiratory disorders, diseases of the nervous and sense organs and senile and pre-senile conditions will have a recognized period where they could require palliative care. This period is less clearly identified for patients with progressive non-malignant diseases than for patients who have cancer.

The data in Table 1 suggest that there may be 6900 people who die from other causes, mainly circulatory or respiratory disorders each year.[9,28]

Although the numbers of people with multiple sclerosis, motor neurone disease and similar disorders are small, these diseases have a much longer duration of symptoms than many of the cancers or other disorders. This factor should be taken into account when planning services.

As for cancer patients the prevalence of symptoms can be used to suggest the numbers who may benefit from palliative care advice, a palliative approach and in some cases specialist services such as hospice or home care.

Prevalence of symptoms and other problems in patients with progressive non-malignant diseases

As for cancer patients the prevalence of symptoms in a random sample of national deaths has been used to calculate the prevalence of symptoms in the population.[8,36-38] These suggest that, among the population of 1 000 000 people, each year 4600 patients with progressive non-malignant diseases have pain, 3400 have trouble with breathing, 1900 have symptoms of vomiting or nausea and 2600 have mental confusion. There are many other symptoms (Table 5).

Table 5: Patients with progressive non-malignant disease: prevalence of problems (per 1 000 000 population)

Symptom	% with symptom in last year of life[a]	Estimated number in each year
Pain	67	4599
Trouble with breathing	49	3363
Vomiting or nausea	27	1853
Sleeplessness	36	2471
Mental confusion	38	2608
Depression	36	2471
Loss of appetite	38	2608
Constipation	32	2196
Bedsores	14	961
Loss of bladder control	33	2265
Loss of bowel control	22	1510
Unpleasant smell	13	892
Total deaths from other causes, excluding accidents, injury and suicide and causes very unlikely to have a palliative period		6864

[a] As per Cartwright and Seale study,[8,36] based on a random sample of deaths and using the reports of bereaved carers.
Note: Patients usually have several symptoms.

High patient anxiety and family distress and anxiety are known to be associated with multiple symptoms, distressing or socially unacceptable symptoms (e.g. unpleasant smell) and poor symptom control. If the prevalences of severe patient anxiety and family anxiety is similar to those among cancer patients, this would suggest that within a population of 1 000 000 severe anxiety would be experienced by approximately 2200 families and 1600 patients.

Estimates based on use of specialist palliative care services by patients with progressive non-malignant diseases

Estimates of the use or need for specialist services among patients with progressive non-malignant diseases are rare. Many specialist palliative services have only recently begun to accept patients who do not have cancer. Services which accept or encourage referrals of patients needing palliative care, irrespective of diagnosis, have reported caseloads where up to one-third or a half have diseases other than cancer.[47,48] Similar figures are found from studies of patients receiving inpatient hospital care.[49] Applying these data to the population would suggest that 350–1400 patients with progressive non-malignant diseases may require a support team for their palliative care and up to 200–700 may require inpatient palliative care (Table 6).

Table 6: Patients with progressive non-malignant diseases: need for specialist palliative services based on local studies of use or need (per 1 000 000 population)[a]

	Number of adults	%
Deaths in one year	6864	
Needing support team	350–1824	0.5–1 times numbers of cancer patients needing care
Needing inpatient palliative care	210–701	0.5–1 times numbers of cancer patients needing care

[a] Studies used include: Hockley *et al.* (1988);[47] Severs and Wilkins (1991);[48] Noble (1993).[49]

People with HIV/AIDS who may need palliative care

Since reporting began in 1982 a total of 10 304 cases meeting the European AIDS case definition were reported in the UK up to the end of December 1994. Of these 7019 were known to have died.[50] The number of deaths has increased over the years; 1065 deaths occurred during 1994 (Table 7). In the same period there were 23 104 laboratory reports of first confirmed HIV-1 antibody positive tests.

Table 7: UK AIDS cases by year of diagnosis and date of known death

Year	Diagnosis	Date of known death
1982 or earlier	17	8
1983	33	15
1984	107	47
1985	240	119
1986	464	270
1987	671	345
1988	884	409
1989	1051	660
1990	1201	772
1991	1340	970
1992	1492	1067
1993	1546	1231
1994	1189	1065
Unknown	69	41
Total	**10304**	**7019**

Source: AIDS/HIV Quarterly Surveillance Tables[50]

Assessing the palliative care needs for people with HIV/AIDS will depend on the underlying prevalence within the population served, the symptoms and problems experienced and the extent to which there is a palliative period. Calculating these is complex. When estimating prevalence in central London, the OPCS death registrations did not prove useful: we found very few cases were identified. Instead data from the Public Heath Laboratory Surveillance appeared to be more accurate.[50] The number of AIDS related deaths varies greatly across the UK and in many populations the numbers are very small. For example, in 1994 it varied from two (Northern Ireland) or eight (Northern Region) to 141 (North West Thames) or 64 (NE Thames).[50] Even within the North East Thames area the number of deaths within health districts in 1993 varied from 0–33 deaths per year.[51] One other district in central London had higher rates than this, with

40–50 HIV/AIDS related deaths per year (personal communication – Kensington & Chelsea and Westminster Health Authority).

The prevalence of symptoms among total populations of people with advancing HIV/AIDS is not well researched. Studies to date have tended to include self-selected samples, such as those patients referred to particular services. However, studies have suggested that the prevalence of symptoms and psychosocial problems in people with HIV/AIDS is as high or higher than among cancer patients, although the nature of many of the symptoms differs. Among patients with advanced HIV/AIDS at least 60% experienced pain[52–54] and over a third needed opioid (e.g. morphine or diamorphine) treatment,[55] 90–100% experienced other symptoms and for 70% these were moderate or severe,[53,54,56] 90–100% experienced anxiety and for 70% this was moderate or severe and at least 50% needed practical support or practical aids.[56] Patients with HIV/AIDS may come from various different cultures and backgrounds which may need quite different support, e.g. for drug users.[57] The natural course of HIV/AIDS includes remissions, acute infections which may require intensive treatment and in some patients the long-term deteriorations associated with HIV/AIDS encephalopathy or cognitive impairment.[52,53,58] Although only a small proportion will develop encephalopathy, those who are affected and their carers need intensive support.[59,61] However the high prevalence of symptoms among people with HIV/AIDS suggests that most would need some palliative support towards the end of life.

Children who may need palliative care

A small proportion of the deaths described on page 192 were among children. Within a population of 1 000 000, if the population is similar to that of the UK,[9,28] there would be approximately 70 deaths in children aged 28 days to four years and 28 among those aged 5–14 years. The majority of these deaths would be due to illnesses or accidents which did not have a palliative period.[9–28] However within a population of this size, current data from England and Wales suggest that approximately three children aged 28 days to four years and five aged 5–14 years would die from cancers. The numbers of children who die from other diseases which may have a palliative period would also be small – two children aged 28 days to four years and one aged 5–14 years from endocrine, nutritional or immune disorders; five aged 28 days to four years and two aged 5–14 years from diseases of the nervous system and senses; and 11 aged 28 days to four years and two aged 5–14 years from congenital disorders.[9,28] Data from OPCS can be used to calculate the exact numbers locally.

Characteristics of patients needing palliative care and local trends

To consider the palliative care for patients within the population in more detail, the OPCS death registration data (page 11) can be analysed to examine:

- the characteristics of those people who will need palliative care in terms of age, sex, etc.
- the trends in place of death over five years
- place of death by electoral ward or locality (five or more years' data should be combined, to avoid very small numbers)
- effect of factors such as social deprivation, ethnicity or services available on place of death.

An example of the results of this for the district of Kensington, Chelsea and Westminster is shown in Appendix IV.

Likely findings would be that there are roughly equal numbers of men and women who died and the rate is constant over the years. The majority of patients who die will be elderly (over 75% will be aged over 65 years and over 50% over 75 years). The majority of deaths will have occurred in hospital (approximately 60–70%) and less at home (24–30%). The number of deaths in hospices will be difficult to calculate from OPCS records because hospices are not coded with a specific category. Free-standing hospices are likely to be coded as 'other communal establishment', hospices within an NHS hospital are likely to be coded as 'NHS hospital' and those hospices operating in private hospitals are likely to be coded as 'private hospital'.

Key issues for health commissioners

Key issues for health commissioners following the analysis of this incidence and prevalence data are as follows. Within a population of 1 000 000 the estimated need for palliative and terminal care is estimated by:

- approximately 2800 cancer deaths each year
- approximately 6900 deaths due to potentially progressive non-malignant disease. Within this there will be three main groups:
  a) those who had a palliative period of advancing, progressive disease
  b) those for whom death was sudden and followed a period where the disease was absent or stable and where they had relatively few symptoms
  c) those for whom there was a chronic disease, where the disease was not clearly progressing, but who might have periods of progression and symptoms where they would benefit from palliative care, and then periods of remission.

This estimates needs as follows:

- approximately 2400 cancer patients will experience pain, 1300 have trouble with breathing and 1400 have symptoms of vomiting or nausea
- approximately 4600 patients with progressive non-malignant diseases have pain, 3400 have trouble with breathing, 1900 have symptoms of vomiting or nausea and 2600 have mental confusion
- if patterns of average national use are followed, 700–1800 cancer patients would require hospital or home palliative care team care and 400–700 should require inpatient hospice or specialist unit care
- if patterns of use where such services exist are followed, up to 350–1800 patients with progressive non-malignant diseases may require a support team for their palliative care and up to 200–700 may require inpatient palliative care
- there may be up to 30 children aged up to 14 years who have a palliative period; most (20) would be under five years of age and half of these would be as a result of congenital disorders. The number of cancer deaths among children would be small – less than ten
- for people with HIV/AIDS the numbers needed in palliative care would depend on the local prevalence of AIDS. Numbers would be nil or small, except in high prevalence areas.

More accurate local estimates can be fairly easily calculated using the data from OPCS death registrations. This would ensure that the estimates take account of local variations within the population.

The commission should also consider the following.

- What proportion of deaths currently occur at home? How does this compare with the national average of 24% and does it vary across the population? How should this influence the way in which services are provided? Variation across the district may mean that some localities need to be targeted for an increase in support services, home nursing or specialist palliative care services.

• What trends have occurred in the place of death for patients – for example over the last ten years – and how might these trends be explained? The development of a hospice or home care service may have impact. Are the percentages of people who die at home increasing or decreasing?

5 Services available

This section outlines palliative care services available for different types of illnesses. The range of clinical and supportive services which should be considered in any district policy for palliative care is described in the following sections. As patterns of provision vary between districts the average national level of use has been included, where available, as indication of availability. These levels of use are not the recommended levels for optimum care.

This section is divided by the sub-categories described on page 9 – underlying type of illness. For each of these the palliative care services and their use is described.

Estimates of service use can be varied throughout the country and may have changed markedly in recent years as the numbers of specialist hospices, units and home care services have expanded. The most comprehensive and up-to-date information on service use is that collected by Addington-Hall and colleagues[37–40] in 1991. This study selected random samples of cancer and non-cancer deaths from death certificates in 20 health districts in the UK and interviewed the nearest carer or family member about the death. It is the largest sample of deaths in this country – and provides information on 2074 cancer deaths and 1622 non-cancer deaths. Many of the findings regarding the prevalence of symptoms and service use were similar to an earlier study in 1987 by Cartwright and Seale,[8,36] except for the use of hospices and specialist services which had increased since that time.

Funding arrangements for the services differ as outlined on page 4. About 75% of hospices and some other specialist palliative care services are organized by voluntary groups.[17] Much of their costs are met by charitable donations with health authorities meeting the remaining costs.

There are difficulties in linking numbers of patients requiring services and the services available. Service activity is often measured in contacts with a range of services some of which are non-NHS. The advent of the NHS number in 1996 onwards will help, although the non-NHS sector will still be omitted.

Cancer

The following list is of palliative care services which provide some degree of palliative care available to people with all types of cancer.

Primary health care

Primary care teams consisting of GP, practice nurse and district nurse provide care for all people in the community and are used by almost all people with cancer in the last year of life (Table 8).

The survey by Addington-Hall *et al.*[37–40] showed that 99% of cancer patients had contact with GPs in their last year of life, but for almost half (43%) this was fewer than ten contacts. Just over a quarter (29%) had over 20 contacts. Although fewer patients (59%) had district nurses when these were available, visits were more frequent – 34% had ten or under visits, 14% 11–20, 26% 21–50 and 27% 51 or more visits in the last year of life.

Some GPs and district nurses have postgraduate training or qualifications in palliative care, symptom control and psychosocial care. Those organizing courses report that high numbers wish to attend and this

Table 8: Use of services by patients in the last year of life. Uses data from Addington–Hall 1993[37–40]

Service	Cancer[b] n = 2074 (%)	Non-cancer[b] n = 1622 (%)
Primary health care		
GP	99	95
Home visit by GP	92	79
Nurses at home	67	36
District nurse	59	32
Health visitor	3	2
Night nursing	19	8
Other community services		
Home help	20	28
Home help if lived alone	40	48
Home help if lived with others	11	16
Meals on wheels if lived alone	22	27
Meals on wheels if lived with others	4	6
Specialist home or hospital palliative care services		
Support team or Macmillan nurses	29	nil
Marie Curie nurses[a]	2	nil
Inpatient care		
Admitted to hospital or hospice	91	72
Hospice		
Hospice inpatient admission	19	<1
Day hospice	3	not available
Spiritual and emotional support		
Chaplains (post-bereavement)	38	34
Support and information groups	11	13
Lived in a nursing or residential home at some point during their last 12 months of life	13	29

[a] Note: In the survey families may not have been able to clearly identify Marie Curie nurses. This finding is disputed by Marie Curie. Data from Marie Curie obtained separately suggest that Marie Curie nurses care for more than one-third of all those who die at home from cancer.
[b] National percentage of people who used the service in their last year of life.

suggests considerable interest and motivation (personal communications from course organizers in the UK). The number who undertake extra training is not known.

Other generic community services

This can include social services such as day care, meals on wheels, home help or home care workers, social workers, laundry and incontinence services, or occupational therapist and other health services such as a health visitor, chiropodist, physiotherapist or clinical nurse specialist from other areas of care, e.g. stoma care. There are also volunteer sitters and workers in many areas and bereavement visitors and support workers.

These services are available in many districts, although to varying extents. Their use by people in the last year of life is fairly limited (Table 8).

Home and hospital specialist palliative care teams and Marie Curie nurses

There are now various forms of services available (see page 7).

Specialist palliative care team (home and hospital)

This team includes doctors, nurses and social workers, although the number in a 'team' can range from 1–11 staff (strictly speaking, one person does not constitute a team). Their function is to provide specialist knowledge in symptom management, control and support, supplement the care of the dying, co-ordinate care, emotional and bereavement support and teaching of staff, carers and patients. They aim to work alongside the primary care team and hospital staff, providing advice and additional support.[1,2]

The teams can be referred to as home care teams and work primarily in the community, or as hospital teams working mainly in hospital. However the boundaries are blurred and many teams will work in both hospital and the community. Teams can be based within a hospice (most common), a hospital, community unit or be independent.

There are over 400 palliative care teams working in hospitals or in the community in the UK and Republic of Ireland[17,62] (Appendix V). Of these about 260 are free standing, community based teams and almost 150 are attached to hospice inpatient units (calculated from[17,62]). Most districts in the UK would have one or more such teams, usually working in a defined catchment area. Just over a quarter of cancer deaths would be cared for by such a service – 57% of patients having help for 1–12 weeks with 2–6 visits per week (Table 8).

Macmillan nurses

Macmillan nurses sometimes work in isolation and sometimes work as part of a palliative care team. Macmillan nurses provide symptom control and support, specialist advice, support, training and liaison with the patient, family and staff involved in caring but do not take over the patient's care. They are self-funding for three to five years after which the district health authority or trust takes over.

Marie Curie nurses

These nurses provide a night and day practical nursing service in patients' homes. There are about 5000 Marie Curie nurses in the UK and they care for about 20 000 patients at home.[5] They are jointly funded by Marie Curie and health authorities. These are not classified as specialist palliative care services.

A survey conducted by the Hospice Information Service showed that in the UK approximately 100 000 patients per year were seen by palliative care nurses. This is over half the number of cancer deaths (160 000) per year.[17,45]

Hospital services

Oncology and radiotherapy services

These offer expert technical facilities and treatment. Treatment may often be given in conjunction with the support care team. The Expert Advisory Group on Cancer to the Chief Medical Officer report on cancer treatment has recommended that cancer treatment centres should be clearly identified and that these should include palliative care.[29]

Hospital inpatient beds

Palliative or terminal care may occur in hospitals for patients who, during their illness have reached the terminal phase of their illness or have been admitted for acute episodes with the possibility of it being the terminal stage and are now comfortable with the hospital as their choice for place of care, and are familiar with the environment and staff. 50% of patients with cancer die in hospital (Table 9).

Table 9: Place of death in 1991 of patients who were identified has having a terminal or palliative period[37-40]

Place of death	Cancer deaths (n = 2074) (%)	Non-cancer deaths (n = 1622) (%)
Home	29	22
Hospital	50	57
Hospice	13	0
Nursing/residential home	7	16
Ambulance/street	0	5

Hospital palliative care teams

These are one form of special palliative care team (see page 204), although in some hospitals there may be only one nurse providing support. This nurse will usually liaise with a community team if patients are discharged. There are now over 250 hospitals in the UK with support teams or support nurses (Appendix V).[17,62]

Hospice

Hospices provide a variety of services including day support, home support teams, night nursing, inpatient units, pain clinics, counselling and training. They admit patients for symptom relief and control, respite and terminal care if the family or patient cannot manage at home.

The Hospice Information Service in 1995 identified 208 units with 3182 beds with various sources of funding,[17,62] (Table 10 and Appendix V). The number of beds in an inpatient hospice unit varied from 2–62.

Table 10: Number and type of inpatient hospice and specialist palliative care services, as of January 1995[17]

Type of inpatient unit	Number of units	Number of beds
Independent or voluntary	142	2196
NHS managed units	46	533
Marie Curie cancer care centres	11	290
Sue Ryder homes	9	163
Total	208	3182

Of cancer deaths Addington-Hall et al. showed that in 1991 19% were admitted to a hospice during some part of the last year of life; 13% died in a hospice.[37-40] A survey conducted by the Hospice Information Service in 1994 suggested that in the UK approximately 28 000 deaths occurred in a hospice.[45] The majority would be cancer patients, so this could represent up to 18% of the 160 000 annual cancer deaths.[45]

Nursing homes and residential homes

Nursing homes and residential homes provide intermittent or continuous respite and continuing care. The NHS tends to take responsibility for individuals who have high nursing needs, while social services combined with the individual take responsibility for others. Many patients already in nursing or residential homes will eventually die there. Nursing homes do not have the specialist facilities of hospices or palliative care teams. Support teams can work with nursing and residential homes (as they work with hospitals or in patients' own homes) to assist and advise in the care of patients who need palliative care.

Other professional services

Pain clinics

These offer pain control and support and are usually run by anaesthetists based in hospitals. The patients are seen in outpatient departments. In 1994 there were over 200 pain clinics operating in the UK.[63] Almost all clinics will accept referrals of malignant pain and chronic pain. A directory of pain clinics was published by the College of Health,[63] and an up-to-date list is available from the Pain Society, British and Irish Chapter of the International Association for the Study of Pain. Pain clinics vary, some being comprehensively staffed and others being very small. Not all clinics will accept GP referrals, some only accept hospital or consultant referrals. Some individuals suggest that the number of patients with cancer pain seen in pain clinics has been reducing in recent years while the number seen with non-malignant pain has increased. This change has sometimes been attributed to the growth of specialist palliative care services for cancer patients (personal communications).

Most districts have dieticians, physiotherapists and occupational therapists who will offer some support for patients dying from cancer although the liaison with the specialist services is varied.

Spiritual and other support

This can be provided by:

- chaplains or other religious leaders, who may work in hospitals, hospices and/or in the local community
- support and information groups and voluntary support organizations run in local hospitals, hospices or palliative care teams by local groups of charities such as Cancer Link. Palliative care teams and hospices have information on most groups being organized locally.

A most useful source of information on local services or contacts is available from the St Christopher's Hospice Information Service (including a directory of services in the UK and Republic of Ireland and information on hospices and services abroad) and the National Council for Hospices and Specialist Palliative Care Services. Leaflets and advice are also available from the BACUP (British Association of Cancer United Patients). Help the Hospices offers education and research support for palliative services or staff and can provide advice.

Other psychological support and alternative therapies are sometimes available such as: aromatherapists, manicurists, beauticians and hairdressers.

Family bereavement support

This is varied and can be provided by:

- social workers – via social services or specialist palliative services and hospices. Social workers are also found in some hospitals
- hospices, support teams who may offer individual support and counselling, organize groups for bereavement and post-bereavement support, or self-help groups
- CRUSE and BACUP are voluntary organizations that also offer support nationally.

Cancer diagnosis specific services

Other care is available from the list below, although this is not confined to palliative patients.

- Clinical nurse specialists e.g. pressure care, continence promotion, nebulizer, Hickman Line nurses for all cancers, chest nurse for cancer of lung, trachea or bronchus and stoma nurse for digestive tract cancer.
- Counsellors for specific groups of patients e.g. mastectomy/breast cancer counsellors for women with breast cancer.

Patients with progressive non-malignant diseases

Very similar services apply for cancer patients as for patients with progressive non-malignant disease although there is less information available. Therefore this section concentrates on the main differences in services.

- **Primary health care** This is used by almost all people with non-cancer in the last year of life (Table 8). Contact is often slightly less than that for cancer patients.
- **Other community services** Services are available in most districts and estimates of use suggested these are used by a higher percentage of non-cancer patients, compared to cancer patients (Table 8).
- **Home and hospital specialist services** Some palliative care teams will accept referrals of patients who do not have cancer. However only a very small proportion of patients are referred to such services (Table 8 shows use in the last year of life). A few teams have a stated policy of accepting all patients but even in these teams the majority of referrals continues to be of cancer patients, with up to 30% of referrals of non-cancer patients.[47,48]
- **Hospital services** Hospital acute ward beds and hospital inpatient beds are important, because about 60% of patients with non-cancer die as hospital inpatients nationally (Table 9).
- **Hospices** 62% of hospices will accept patients who do not have cancer but require palliative care.[62] Reports suggest that hospices are used by very few people who do not have cancer (Tables 8 and 9).
- **Nursing homes** These are increasingly common as a place of care and death in the last year of life, especially among elderly and frail patients (Table 9).
- **Pain clinics** These play an increasing role in the care of patients with advanced non-malignant diseases for pain control and support.
- **Other psychological support and alternative therapies** For example aromatherapists, manicurists, beauticians and hairdressers are available in many hospices and occasionally in hospitals or long-term care facilities.

Additional services for non-cancer patients

The following additional services are available to people with specific non-cancer terminal illnesses. Most are not confined to people who need palliative care.

Hereditary degenerative disorder

For example muscular dystrophy.

- genetic counselling support and information services
- family support groups and support and information groups – voluntary.

Dementia

- community care assistants
- sitting services for respite for carers
- domiciliary home services including mental health teams for elderly people, Admiral nurses (funded by the charity Dementia Relief and working to support the family), community psychiatric nurses
- home help daily personal care with: hygiene, eating, pensions, shopping, cleaning
- incontinence laundry service – social services
- special beds in nursing homes
- hospital wards for people with dementia. Many long stay wards seek to provide homely care in small units. There is at least one hospital which has converted a house and developed a 'hospice like' model of care for people with dementia. However this is the exception
- voluntary support and information groups and associations for carers and for people with dementia
- charities such as the Alzheimer's Disease Society and the Mental Health Foundation provide information, have support groups in some areas and support research
- co-ordinators to inform carers of services that are available and how to access them.

Circulatory disease

- support and information groups in some areas
- advice and leaflets, plus support groups in some areas via the British Heart Foundation or via stroke groups.

Cystic fibrosis

- specialist community nursing service enabling a family to care for their child at home in the terminal phase of their illness
- hospices for children accept this condition. There are few hospices for children (page 27)
- cystic fibrosis physiotherapists
- genetic advice for cystic fibrosis
- parental and family support, information and counselling, including bereavement counselling are available in some districts.

Motor neurone disease and multiple sclerosis

- hospices – almost all hospices will admit people with motor neurone disease and multiple sclerosis if they have far advanced disease or for respite care
- there are special support groups and associations for people with motor neurone disease and multiple sclerosis and their families available from the voluntary sector.

Services for people with HIV/AIDS

Existing social and health services are available together with some of the services described for patients with cancer. Services specializing in support for people with HIV/AIDS can be found, particularly in high prevalence areas. These include the following.

- **Other community services** Advocacy workers, voluntary services including Buddy schemes, Terrence Higgins Trust and volunteers organized from local groups or hospices.
- **Specialist services** These may be:
  a) special AIDS teams – multi-professional teams similar to the home support team for cancer patients which may care for people with AIDS are found in areas where AIDS is most common e.g. London districts
  b) home support teams for cancer patients which may care for people with AIDS/HIV
  c) clinical nurse specialists who are found in many districts, especially where AIDS/HIV is common. They offer advice for patients with HIV/AIDS at all stages of the illness.
- **Hospital services** Beds reserved for people with AIDS.
- **Hospices** Many hospices will accept people with HIV or AIDS, although in some instances only when the person has a cancer-like illness. Inpatient and day care services specifically for people with HIV/AIDS are found especially in places where HIV/AIDS is common, for example in the London area, London Lighthouse, Mildmay Mission Hospital and, offering residential care for people with HIV/AIDS related encephalopathy, Patrick House.

Terminal illnesses in children

Children with terminal illnesses and their families receive the following additional services in some areas.

Mobile specialist services

Specialist community nursing service can enable families to care for their child at home in the terminal phase of their illness. Many of the teams caring for adults will care for children, but there are a few specialist teams which deal only with children from children's hospitals, e.g. Gt Ormond Street, London.

Hospice/inpatient

Children's hospices are available in a few areas. The Association for Children with Life Threatening or Terminal Conditions and their Families (ACT) lists eight established and ten planned hospices for children in England. The established hospices are:

- Acorns, Birmingham (ten beds)
- Derian House, Rochester, Lancashire (nine beds)
- Francis House, Manchester (seven beds)
- Helen House, Oxford (eight beds)
- Martin House, Wetherby, West Yorkshire (nine beds)
- Quidenham Children's Hospice, Norfolk (six beds)
- Rainbows Children's Hospice, Loughborough, Leicestershire (eight beds)
- Children's Hospice, Milton, Cambridgeshire (12 beds).

Those planned are:

- Hope House, Oswestry, Shropshire
- Children's Hospice Association Scotland, Edinburgh
- Children's Hospice South West, Barnstaple, Devon
- Claire House, Liverpool, Merseyside
- Demelza House, Rochester, Kent
- Little Haven, Southend-on-Sea, Essex
- Rainbow House, Walsall
- Richard House Appeal, Canning Town, London
- Ty Hafan Appeal, Barry, Glamorgan
- Wessex Children's Hospice Trust.

In addition to inpatient care most of the hospices offer home care services, hospice at home, day care and/or respite care.

Other professional services

Other professional services may include psychosocial support from clinical psychologists and social workers, specialist paediatric oncology nurses to improve communication between patient and family and patient and health care workers.

Charities

Charities such as Dreams Come True and the Starlight Foundation provide special treats and holidays for terminally ill children.

6 Effectiveness and cost-effectiveness of therapies and services

This section reviews the effectiveness and cost-effectiveness of therapies and services used in palliative care. Following the guidelines for these needs assessments of Stevens and Raftery[21] the quality of the evidence and strength of recommendation for each procedure are graded (see Appendix VI for grades).

Effectiveness in palliative care is judged in terms of the quality of life before dying, quality of life at the time of dying, a 'good death' and the impact on the family or carers. These can include elements such as the control of pain and symptoms, relief of psychosocial or emotional problems for the patient or family, subsequent resolution of grief and in some cases the achievement of particular wishes, such as developing a new interest or activity.

Efficacy and cost-effectiveness of individual therapies and treatments

There is a large body of work which assesses the efficacy of drug therapies and interventions in these patients (for detailed reviews and summaries, see many of the available textbooks, including *The Management of Terminal Malignant Disease*[3] and the *Oxford Textbook of Palliative Medicine*[64]). It is not appropriate to describe this in detail, but some of the common recommendations follow.

Pain and symptom control

The management of pain requires a detailed assessment.[3,64] There are many different types of pain. Ev...
has demonstrated that, in particular, cancer patients will have several different pains, each with a diff...
cause.[65] The prevalence of and the ability to control the pain is related to its aetiology.[66] The World Hea...
Organization (WHO) has recommended a regimen for the treatment of morphine-sensitive pain, which
advocates that drugs should be given a) orally, b) regularly according to the half-life of the drug and c)
following the WHO analgesic 'ladder', which moves from non-opioid (morphine-like) drugs to weak opioids
to strong opioids.[67–68]

Quality of the evidence is (I) – large multicentre and randomized controlled trials have demonstrated that
cancer pain can be controlled in the majority of patients,[3,64,67–71] strength of recommendation (A).
Improvements in the use of the analgesic ladder and its use for different types of pain is being further
researched.

There is good evidence that there are also types of pain that are only partially (or not at all) responsive
to morphine.[67–72] These include pains due to the spread of the cancer to the bone, and pains due to
destruction of nerve tissue. There are many other adjuvant therapies for these particular types of pain
including non-steroid anti-inflammatory drugs, steroids, anticonvulsant, antispasmodic, anti-arrhythmic
and anti-depressant drugs.[68–73] Radiotherapy, surgery, neural blockade and other physical measures
(e.g. transcutaneous nerve stimulation, acupuncture) and psychosocial interventions also may have a role.
Evaluations of these therapies are under way and reviews of effectiveness of treatments such as non-steroidal
anti-inflammatory drugs are available.[73] Therefore the management of pain in terminal illness is complex and
in a proportion of patients requires specialized assessment.[68,72] This area remains under investigation.
However quality of the evidence for the use of adjuvants, if indicated, is (II-1) and given the need to control
symptoms, if the WHO ladder is insufficient, the strength of recommendation is (A). Specialist advice may
be needed to ensure that up–to–date treatments are given. The National Council for Hospice and Specialist
Palliative Care Services has recently published straightforward clinical guidelines for pain control in
palliative care.[68]

The control of other symptoms is similarly complex and often requires specialized knowledge.
Evaluations of the drug therapies and interventions is fairly well established and comprehensive reviews of
their efficacy are available.[74–77]

The delivery system of drugs has been revolutionized during the last decade and in particular studies it has
been shown that the delivery of some analgesics and anti-emetics (anti-sickness) drugs subcutaneously using
a battery-operated pump[66,78] has enabled people to be cared for at home when otherwise they might require
hospital treatment. The most notable example of this is the management of patients with gastro-intestinal
obstruction where it was demonstrated that this simple treatment was as effective and often better than the
previous treatment, which involved inserting a naso-gastric tube and removing the contents of the stomach
by suction, and inserting an intravenous line and providing fluids by that route.[79,80] Quality of the evidence is
(II-2 and II-3), patients can be involved in the choice of delivery system and the evidence of the efficacy of the
drugs is (I) as above. Therefore strength of recommendation is (A).

Few studies have compared the costs of these recommended treatments. There are two possible reasons
for this. First the control of symptoms is often considered to be an essential requirement in care. Second
many of the therapies, for example morphine, diamorpine or delivery systems with battery-operated syringe
drivers, are relatively inexpensive, especially if compared with an extended inpatient stay due to
uncontrolled symptoms. These therapies are also in line with moves towards 'appropriate technologies' as
suggested by the WHO in their primary health care programme,[81] in that the treatments and technologies are
relatively cheap, simple and can be used away from the hospital.

Emotional support and communication

Emotional support is a common desire by some patients and their families and communication is one of the most common concerns expressed by patients and families. There have been frequent complaints that doctors and nurses do not provide sufficient information about the diagnosis and are not well skilled at talking to patients and families.[44,82-85] There is some evidence (quality II-2 and II-3) that hospices and specialist palliative care services are successful in meeting emotional needs (page 31). In 1985 Lunt demonstrated that two hospices met emotional needs as well as those concerning anxiety, depression and physical symptoms better than a district general hospital.[86]

Co-ordination

Co-ordination is also a frequent concern; many patients and families complain of poor co-ordination of services. There are various ways of addressing this problem, and often Macmillan or support team nurses have a significant role in co-ordinating services. There is some evidence (quality = II-2 and II-3) that they are successful in this role.[43,86]

However the model of an extra independent co-ordinating service was not found helpful in one randomized controlled trial. Two co-ordinating nurses did not appear to have any benefits over and above existing conventional and specialized palliative care services.[87] Therefore there is fair evidence not to utilize this type of 'special' co-ordinating service (level D).

Bereavement

Bereavement and grief for carers is known to be a risk factor for increased mortality and ill health, particularly among elderly men.[88] Risk assessment tools to identify those patients at highest risk of prolonged grief are available[89] and there is some evidence that such support is welcomed by bereaved relatives, but this is patchy. (Quality of evidence = II-2, II-3 and III, strength of recommendation B.) However, the proportion of families requiring bereavement follow-up is currently disputed[89] and bereavement support is known to vary greatly.[90]

Effectiveness of conventional care

During the 1970s and 1980s many studies demonstrated deficiencies in conventional care for dying people both in hospitals and the community. Dying patients suffered severe unrelieved symptoms particularly pain, had unmet practical, social and emotional needs and suffered as the result of poor co-ordination of services and because health professionals appeared unwilling to share information.[91-94] In hospital staff were observed to withdraw from patients and to pay little attention to their symptoms, emotional needs or needs for care.[94]

Their families also suffered because of poor communication by health professionals and had unmet needs for emotional, practical and bereavement support.[84-86,93,95,96] Cancer patients were found to have depression and anxiety more commonly than in the 'normal' population, while their families also were at risk of developing social and psychiatric problems.[97]

Attention shifted to home care when further work emphasized the increased severity of many problems while the patient was at home, where the patient spent most of their time.[98,99] Also studies have estimated that 50–70% of cancer patients would prefer to be cared for or to die at home.[100,101] A longitudinal study of patients in the care of a domiciliary palliative care team suggested that as death approached patients changed their preferences: hospital and home became less preferred and hospice more preferred, although even one week before death 50% still wished to be cared for at home.[102] However far fewer achieve this and the number of people who die at home has fallen in recent years (from 42% in 1969 to 24% in 1987).[8] 29% of cancer deaths included in the Regional Study of Care for the Dying (RSCD) by Addington-Hall *et al.* died at home.[40] The RSCD, which examined care in the last year of life for random samples of cancer and non-cancer deaths, demonstrated continued problems of unrelieved pain and other symptoms and that relatives bore the brunt of caring.[40]

Therefore the quality of evidence that conventional care alone failed to meet the needs of many patients and families was strong (quality of evidence = II-1, II-2, II-3 and III) and there is poor evidence to support the use of conventional care alone (level D).

Effectiveness and cost-effectiveness of specialist palliative services compared with conventional care

Hospices and specialist palliative teams were developed to try and fill the deficiencies described in conventional services. However there are very few randomized controlled trials of these services. Evidence for the different services is summarized as follows.

Inpatient hospices

Controlled and comparative studies of inpatient hospices versus other forms of inpatient care have suggested that the hospice model is at least as effective as conventional models of care in terms of the management of pain and symptoms. In some instances it has shown benefits in terms of symptom control, anxiety, depression and bereavement outcome and it has nearly always shown benefits in terms of patient and family satisfaction with care. Quality of evidence ranges from I – but note that the randomized controlled and multi-centre trials were in North America and have not been repeated in the UK – to III. Most of the services evaluated accepted exclusively or mainly cancer patients. Therefore, the strength of recommendation is (B/A), for reviews of studies see.[2,94,103–114] Multi-centre studies of the effectiveness and costs of inpatient hospices, especially in the care of patients with progressive non-malignant diseases are needed.

There is also evidence that hospices use a higher number of nursing staff per patient than conventional care, but use fewer invasive therapeutic procedures and investigations.[104,105,115] The costs of inpatient hospice care versus conventional care suggest that hospice care is similar to or cheaper than conventional care.[94,106,116,117] However all but one of these studies are from North America, which has a very different health system compared with the UK. There is little information on comparison costs in the UK. Because when setting contracts with voluntary hospices the NHS does not have to cover the full costs, while this arrangement continues voluntary hospices can represent very good value for NHS commissioners. The costs of inpatient hospice care vary considerably from hospice to hospice. Hill and Oliver[118,119] demonstrated that very small hospices had higher costs, but also a higher throughput when compared with larger hospices. They recommended that the optimal size of a hospice, in general, was 15 beds or larger.

Hospices do vary considerably in their activity, types of staffing and procedures undertaken.[120–122] Organizational standards have been developed by various bodies including the Royal College of Physicians[123] by a Delphi exercise of participating experts,[124] NAHAT,[26] the Royal College of Nursing[125] and by the Cancer Relief Macmillan Fund, which later became an organizational audit programme.[126] These include guidelines on the nature and training of hospice doctors and nurses, and the environment and nature of services. They are based on the opinions of those experts on the panels and some aspects of all the standards agree – e.g. use of staff trained in specialist palliative care etc. However, they are rarely well referenced and their use has not been evaluated. Therefore the quality of evidence for these organizational standards is III. Research is needed to compare the effects of different hospices, before details of the most effective structure of care delivery is known.

Specialist palliative care teams and specialist advice

A wide range of different structures and processes of specialist palliative care teams has developed. Teams commonly work most closely with or within the NHS, offering shared care, advice and support by working alongside GPs and hospital staff. Teams were often originally planned by district health authorities either independently or in conjunction with the charity the Cancer Relief Macmillan Fund, which pump-primed posts, providing the trust and/or district health authority took over funding after three to five years.[7] However a 'team' can vary in size from one nurse to 11 nurses and may have doctors, social workers and in some cases a chaplain, occupational therapist, physiotherapist, psychologist, dietician, administrator or secretary.[7] Catchment populations have been found to range from 43 000 to 500 000 per 'team', with variations in the nurse caseload from 11 to 57 current patients per nurse.[7,127] One team may offer both home care and hospital support. Teams usually confine their remit to advice and emotional support and the nursing members do not provide 'hands on' nursing care: this is carried out by existing services.

Some of the larger, multi-professional home care teams have been evaluated in randomized controlled trials and various other comparative studies. The home care teams were able to demonstrate their ability to keep patients at home for longer than when such services did not exist. They also resulted in lower costs to the health service (between 18% to eight times lower costs than inpatient care) and in equivocal or improved pain control,[2,43,106–107,109–111,116,117,128–137] except for one comparative study which suggested that relatives reported more pain in patients kept at home compared with those in hospital.[99] Much of the cost data are from North America rather than the UK. All studies showed higher patient satisfaction in home care teams compared to conventional care.[2,85,99,129,131,135] A study comparing patient satisfaction with home care teams, GPs and hospital services demonstrated that patients were more satisfied with the home care team than with their GP and district nurses and least satisfied with the hospital service.[85]

Therefore there is strong evidence that adding a multi-professional support team can provide a higher quality care than conventional care alone: quality of evidence = I (note again the randomized controlled trials were in North America and not in the UK), II-1, II-2, II-3 and III. Some of the services did care for patients with progressive non-malignant diseases, and in one cost-effectiveness study for HIV/AIDS.[137] There is good evidence to support its use (level A).

Studies which compare the different types of teams, for example larger multi-professional teams with smaller teams comprising only nurses are not available. One study has reported better symptom control for a team approach comprising GP, district nurse and specialist palliative nurse, compared to GPs operating alone.[138] Otherwise, the nurse–only teams have not been rigorously evaluated.

Harper *et al.* showed that a consensus of palliative care doctors and nurses favoured multi-professional teams rather than nurse-only teams.[124] Other reports have also recommended a multi-professional approach.[68,123,126]

Hospital support services

The evaluation of hospital support teams is less well evolved than that of other services. However there have been a few studies that have demonstrated the effectiveness of the service in terms of its ability to assist in the control of symptoms and have reported that patients and families have benefited from the service.[36,43,47,139] Again the evaluations have mainly considered the larger multi-professional teams rather than single-handed nurses. (Quality of evidence = II-3 and III, strength of recommendation B, although further research is needed.)

Day care

Day care has been largely unevaluated and varies considerably throughout the country. It can be offered as part of an inpatient hospice service or associated with a home care team, or both. Research into the effectiveness, appropriateness and costs of day care is urgently needed before further growth occurs.

Practical support and respite care

There is also some evidence to demonstrate that practical and respite support is needed by patients and carers and the provision of this is patchy throughout the country. In 1991 Addington-Hall and colleagues advocated the transfer of funds from acute hospital services to community-based services.[44] The provision of practical and respite support for palliative carers remains largely unresolved.[140,141] Such support is not usually provided by mobile support teams. There is also anecdotal evidence that many 'respite' admissions to hospices are too late in the course of illness and carry a distinct mortality.

In some instances, the provision of respite care is met by inpatient hospices but the provision of practical support at home is an issue for many patients and families. To assist this, in many areas hospices also run teams of volunteers to provide an additional sitting service, as does the Marie Curie Cancer Care Service. Evaluation of a relative support team, which was part funded by Marie Curie Cancer Care showed high satisfaction among relatives.[142]

Hospice at home

A new model of care has developed recently which seeks to combine the specialist advice of specialist palliative care services (which do not usually provide hands-on nursing care), existing district nursing services and practical support, in terms of nursing, sitting and basic care, at home.[143] The care offered is very like that of hospital at home,[144] but with specialist palliative support from the local hospice or home care team added. This service is usually called hospice at home, but note that two services which operate in a similar way to home care support teams and do not offer practical nursing care at home, have already called themselves hospice at home.

Hospital at home was shown to benefit terminally ill patients in a comparative trial.[144] Therefore this development of hospice at home appears promising. At least two pilot schemes are under way and are in the process of evaluation. One scheme was developed in an area where there was no existing night or day sitting/nursing service generally available. It was specifically geared towards patients with advanced HIV/AIDS where Marie Curie nurses could not be used. Early data from this scheme, which was led by a consultant in palliative medicine, suggested that the proportion of patients cared for at home was increased and that symptoms were controlled. A more detailed evaluation is planned.[143]

Social variations

Eight-fold differences in the proportions of cancer patients dying at home have been found between areas of high and low deprivation, suggesting that this has an impact on care.[145]

Services for patients with progressive non-malignant diseases and HIV/AIDS

Studies which demonstrated failings in conventional care included cancer and non-cancer patients. Patients also appear to have a poorer quality of care if they are of lower social class.[146] However there is little evaluation of new services for patients with progressive non-malignant diseases. This may be partly because specialist care for these patients is rare and partly because the teaching and textbooks which consider the care for patients with these diseases frequently omit the palliative aspects. A randomized controlled trial of a mobile palliative care team demonstrated benefits for elderly patients, whatever their condition.[128] The evaluation of the hospital teams has also assessed the care of non-cancer patients.[47] Severs and Wilkins described how they were able to convert part of a ward caring for elderly people into one which provided inpatient palliative care and successfully cared for elderly people, where 79% had cancers and 21% other diseases.[48] (Quality of evidence = I and III.) Expansion of home care teams to include more patients with non-cancer diagnoses has shown increased cost savings.[147]

Evaluations have also demonstrated that the model of hospice and home support can be successfully transferred to care for patients with HIV/AIDS, although some symptoms are more common or have different presentations.[136,137,148–150] General practitioners have also indicated that they would like extra support and advice for terminally ill patients with all diseases,[151–155] although studies have found that some GPs were unaware of the local services available or did not know how to refer to a palliative service.[154]

What proportion of patients and families experience a palliative period, with what characteristics and nature of problems that would benefit most from these types of service needs further study.

Services for children

Many of the specialist palliative care teams and hospital support teams described will care for children and their families.[17,62] However the numbers of children cared for are small and no evaluations are available. Descriptive studies of hospices are available but these do not include an evaluative component. Evaluation is made difficult by the small numbers of children cared for. Hospices for children are subject to much debate, and experts disagree on whether such services should be supported.[156,157] Research into the needs of children and their families and the effectiveness of models of care is needed.

Key issues

For a health authority considering the data on effectiveness key issues in relation to their services would be as follow.

- Strength of recommendations for multi-disciplinary palliative home care teams is A and for inpatient hospices is B/A. The recommendation for hospital teams is B. Conventional care alone within a district is inadequate.

   Do the methods of staffing, size and methods of working of the specialist palliative services concord with those types of services which have been demonstrated to be effective, cost-effective and efficient? Other specialist palliative care developments need to be evaluated as they are introduced.
- Are the services offering a multi-professional approach, as is generally recommended?
- Are there mechanisms for co-ordination of care between NHS, voluntary and social services – is this carried out by palliative care teams, do they work and can they be improved – given that this is often considered to be one of the major problems for patients and families nationally?
- Given that many patients will not be cared for in specialist palliative settings, what are the systems for educating and insuring staff are sufficiently trained in the palliative aspects of care such as the correct range of techniques for pain and symptom control, emotional support, staff with good communication skills and bereavement care?
- Given that many more patients wish to be cared for at home or to die at home than currently achieve this, what alteration in mix of services would be needed to increase the proportion of people who can be offered palliative care at home?

7 Models of care

This section sets out models of palliative provision which are indicated by the previous sections on prevalence, incidence, effectiveness and service provision. A range of levels of service provision is given – these levels will depend on the components included.

Cancer patients

A cost-effective programme for palliative care would include the following.

- Multi-professional home care and hospital support for 25–60% of cancer deaths.
- Inpatient hospice care for approximately 15–30% of cancer deaths. Very small units, i.e. less than 10–15 beds, should be avoided if possible because of their higher costs when compared with larger hospices. The nature of the service provided by the hospice should be multi-professional, with a high nurse–patient ratio and medical staff trained in palliative medicine, as suggested by the current standards. (This may need to be amended when better data of the most effective structure of care are available.)
- An education programme and quality standards for hospital and community staff who care for patients with advanced cancer – including symptom control, communication, patient and family referral and information on appropriate services.
- Quality standards which would probably include the development of clinical protocols for the management and referral, where appropriate, of patients and families with particular problems or symptoms. Protocols for symptoms and pathologies would be based on therapies which have known efficacy.
- Local systems which should be developed to provide hospital and community staff with information about the palliative services available locally. Each district may have knowledge about the systems which will work best, but in some areas GPs have complained about excessive distribution of paper. In these cases a small, short 'placemat' of services would be appropriate.[158] Other districts have found short directories were useful.[159]
- Developments in day care, hospice at home or additional home support may be needed locally, especially if districts wish to increase the proportion of patients cared for at home. However these should only occur as part of evaluative studies, preferably comparative studies, which include details of costs. Also the multi-professional home care and hospital support and inpatient hospice care might effectively be expanded, but if this occurs development should be evaluated to determine the costs, numbers of patients cared for and effects, including the impact on acute hospital care.
- Audit and monitoring of the outcomes of care in all settings.
- Quality standards agreed between purchasers and providers would be needed to ensure the integration of services and good co-ordination across all sectors.

Patients with other diseases

- Existing specialist palliative care services should be encouraged to take patients who have diseases other than cancer which require palliative care, up to one-third or one-half of their workload. Their involvement should be audited and evaluated.
- Education, training and quality standards should be developed for all settings where palliative care is needed and these should be monitored through audit. These might include the development of clinical protocols for the management and referral, where appropriate, of patients and families with particular problems or symptoms, as above. Protocols would need more testing than that for cancer patients, above,

because there are less data on the efficacy of palliative treatments. All settings where palliative care occurs should be included in this (section 5). Note that an increasing proportion of patients remain in nursing, residential and warden aided homes until their death and that these settings too may need specialist palliative advice, support and training.

These services should be encouraged to call for specialist advice when caring for more complex patients and families.

- Other service developments, mechanisms for providing information about local services, audit and outcomes, should as much as possible be integrated into the existing arrangements for cancer patients. These should also include those services already caring for many non-cancer patients with advancing disease, as described in section 5.

Services for children

- The small numbers within many health districts and the lack of evaluative information suggest that districts should ensure that existing palliative support services, especially the mobile community teams, will include care, advice and support for children and their families.
- Specialist teams from tertiary referral centres, e.g. the Great Ormond Street Team, may be used to support and advise the local palliative care teams, if appropriate.
- Hospices for children should be developed only if these are part of a rigorous evaluation. Alternatively, it may be argued that the existing hospices for children require evaluation, along with a better assessment of children's and families' wishes for care, before any further developments are supported.

Different models

Having carried out the needs assessment, the options for a population might be as follow.

- To move towards increasing community support in palliative care, perhaps by increasing the input of specialist home care support teams or developing hospice at home models. This might be particularly appropriate in areas where few patients are able to be cared for at home. Note that any hospice at home development would need evaluation.
- To increase the inpatient hospice care. This might be a very attractive choice, if there are few patients currently cared for within hospices, particularly if there are local voluntary hospices where the health authority does not have to fund the full costs. There may be hospices with unused capacity, or they may wish to develop more hospice beds. Note, however, that this relationship would depend on the continued availability of voluntary funding. NHS hospices are likely to have similar costs to NHS hospitals and are often considered preferable; therefore NHS hospices may also be an attractive option for a health authority.
- To move away from providing specialist palliative care and try to incorporate this with all generic services. There is no research evidence to support such a move, nor is there evidence that without specialist palliative care services generic services improve by themselves.
- To increase the emphasis of the specialist palliative care services on education programmes. This might be an option for health authorities which already have a provision of specialist palliative care but which they feel is rather isolated from existing services and is not providing any educational input. This would also be an option for districts wishing to improve the care for patients who do not have cancer, without significantly increasing the resources to specialist palliative care services.
- To increase the hospital support through hospital palliative care teams. This may be an option for populations where there is no current hospital support and many patients are dying within hospitals.

Examples from other districts

Assessments of need from other districts and countries have included analysis of incidence and prevalence, but usually of only cancer patients, and analysis of local opinions, activity or trends.[46,158,160–162,170] In some instances districts have undertaken special surveys.[46,163–169] The study by Addington-Hall included 20 health districts, each of whom have been given local data, to provide them with better information on the characteristics and needs of patients and their families.[37–40,171] An example of a service specification from one district, which includes details of some of the quality aspects and their monitoring, is shown in Appendix VII.

A health authority may wish to determine how the estimates of incidence, prevalence of symptoms and likely numbers of patients needing care relate to local provision in terms of completed episodes, new referrals or spending on different services.

In 1990 Frankel[46] undertook a needs assessment for the Bristol area and concluded that approximately 50 inpatient hospice beds were required for a population of one million. This was based on the estimates of GPs and hospital staff on the number of patients with cancer who would require palliative care. Kensington & Chelsea and Westminster Health Authority undertook a survey of GPs, to obtain their views about the appropriate direction of palliative care and found that they were particularly concerned about the availability of 24-hour support.[154] A survey of district health authorities in England identified 67 which had planned or completed reviews of palliative care services.[170]

Further examples from the National Council for Hospice and Specialist Palliative Care Services

The National Council for Hospice and Specialist Palliative Care Services has produced guidance on setting contracts, describing services and assessing need. Although much of the information in this document is rather general it does contain examples of needs assessments and contracting experiences.[172] They have published further information for purchasers, to provide a background for available specialist palliative care services.[24] This provides an up-to-date and detailed description of the type of staff, services and modes of operating which are found and are recommended for specialist palliative care services.[24] This report is accompanied by another providing details of outcome measures[173] and their uses in palliative care, which expands on the following section of this chapter. They have also published a statement of definitions of specialist palliative care services.[22]

8 Outcome measures

Palliative care cannot be measured with commonly used outcome measures such as mortality or disability, but requires measurement of aspects which are important to patients with progressive disease and their families. It therefore deals with the quality of life, quality of death and dying and the bereavement outcome. Examples of the aspects of care within these three areas which might be measured by outcomes are shown in Box 1. Clearly outcomes may reflect positive or adverse events within the area of care; although most of the available outcome measures tend to measure the presence, absence or degree of problems, such as pain, anxiety, symptoms, rather than positive events such as fulfilment in life.

Box 1: Examples of aspects for outcome measurement in palliative care

---

General areas

- quality of life – all aspects, physical, emotional, social, spiritual
- quality of dying – all aspects as for quality of life including resolving last issues, planning
- bereavement outcome

Specific examples

- control of pain and symptoms
- relief of anxieties and fears for patient and family
- meet wishes for place of care and death (e.g. at home)
- meet needs for practical care, financial help
- patient and family feel that the communication and information given have been given as they would wish
- last wishes before death are met – e.g. meeting with estranged family
- satisfaction with care
- relief of depression
- lessened mortality and morbidity during bereavement

Quality of life measures or adaptations of these measures are often used to assess outcomes in palliative care. Early definitions of quality of life concentrated on physical function. Then these were extended to include symptoms of the disease, emotional and psychological functioning. Most recently aspects of social functioning, sexual needs and spiritual needs have been added.[174,175] Although the definition of quality of life currently lacks a consensus, the commonly identified domains include:[173–176]

- physical concerns (e.g. symptoms, pain, etc.)
- functional ability (activity, self-care)
- emotional well-being, psychological function
- social functioning
- occupational functioning
- spirituality
- sexuality (including body image)
- treatment satisfaction
- financial concerns
- future plans/orientation (hope, planning)
- family well-being – emotional and physical.

Measuring palliative care outcomes within other national outcomes initiatives

Some measures of outcome are being set nationally. One relevant to palliative care is pressure sores. The NHS Executive 1994/95 Planning Guidance stated that health authorities should ensure that contracts specify that providers record the incidence and prevalence of pressure sores 'differing between those acquired in hospital and others', and are 'encouraged to set annual targets for an overall reduction of at least 5% working from a baseline 1993/94 figures'. A guide on pressure sore measurement, risk assessment and management has been published[177] and these measures are being monitored in hospices throughout the country.

The results of this measurement need to be adjusted for the characteristics of patients receiving palliative care. Patients who are weak and close to the end of life are often at a high risk of developing pressure sores. Also it is difficult in such debilitated patients to know if they have a 'true' pressure sore, or if it is tumour eroding the skin. The results from some settings have shown that patients arrive in the hospice unit having already acquired pressure sores (personal communications). The management of pressure sores must also be viewed within the context of a patient's complete care and the distress caused by the pressure sore, rather than simply its size.

Some difficulties in outcome measurement in palliative care

Case-mix and attributability

The patients and families who receive palliative care are not a homogenous group but have different diagnoses and aetiologies of symptoms and problems which have varying prognoses. For example in many instances a patient's pain(s) are relatively easy to control, but some are not, especially neuropathic pains. Therefore where possible the results of outcome measurement need to be adjusted for case-mix – especially if these are likely to be different, e.g. in an inpatient hospice versus a hospital ward. Similarly it is difficult to be certain that the intervention affected the change in outcome, outside the context of a randomized controlled trial.

Accounting for individual wishes

Patients vary in their individual wishes for care while they are dying and these wishes may change over time, depending upon a person's experiences. For example, although many patients wish to die at home, a substantial proportion do not.[100-102] Although some patients wish for close communication with their family or for spiritual support when they are close to death, others do not.[3,82,83] Therefore when measuring outcomes it is important to try to ensure that these reflect the wishes of individual patients and families.[178] This is often not easy, especially with standard instruments which are designed for use in populations and when patients and families have different wishes or expectations.

Accounting for differences between patient, family and professional assessments and wishes

Patients, their family, professionals and external assessors have all been used to assess outcomes in different ways. The main advantages and drawbacks of using the different assessors are considered in detail elsewhere.[179] There is probably no ideal choice of assessor and it is best to choose who is most appropriate for the setting being considered and the way in which the outcomes will be used.

Measures which can be used to assess outcome

Outcome measures are being tested among patients and families who need palliative care. These include the Support Team Assessment Schedule[32,178,179] and the Edmonton Symptom Assessment System,[180] both of which were designed for the quick assessment of outcomes in clinical practice. The first of these was developed in the UK in community settings, the second was developed in Canada in inpatient settings. Both are now used in many countries and in both inpatient and community settings. Measures developed for research are also being tested and adapted for use as outcome measures. These include the measures of quality of life developed for cancer patients, such as the Rotterdam Symptom Checklist[181] and the European Organisation for Research into Quality of Life Instrument,[182] and psychosocial measures such as the Hospital Anxiety and Depression Scale.[183] Details of these measures are shown in Table 11.

Other approaches to assessing the quality of care

Other approaches to the assessment of the quality of palliative care have developed. They include the Cancer Relief Macmillan Fund Organisational Audit, which provides a method to examine the organizational structure in which palliative care is offered. This is described in detail elsewhere.[125] It provides a framework and programme of inspection which purchasers and providers may wish to examine or adapt to their own circumstances.[125] More sophisticated assessments of the process of care than simply assessing the number of visits could also be used. This might involve assessing the way that staff work with patients and families, their communication skills or observing the interactions which take place.[94] Some health authorities have monitored the percentage of patients who die at home as a very crude indicator.

9 Targets

Health gain targets can be developed to improve the control of pain and symptoms and the relief of anxieties, and service targets to ensure service delivery in these areas. Examples are shown below.

Health gain targets

Targets suitable for national monitoring

- The percentage of cancer patients who are cared for or die at home, in a hospice or specialist palliative care unit.
- The percentage of patients receiving specialized palliative care – including all settings: home, hospital, residential, hospice.

Local targets

- Increase the proportion of patients and families who report their pain and symptoms are controlled, or that symptoms do not affect them. (Note: the prevalence of symptoms may not be affected but the success of control and the degree to which symptoms affect the patient may be reduced.)
- Increase the proportion of patients and families who feel that communication from health staff has met their requirements.
- Increase the proportion of patients and families who are cared for in the place of their choice.
- Reduce the mortality and morbidity following bereavement.
- Increase the satisfaction of patients and families with the palliative care provided.

Table 11: Some outcome measures which have been used, or are proposed for use, in palliative care

Name and source	Number of items and domains included	How developed and setting	Comments on use
Rotterdam symptom checklist[181]	34 symptoms covering: physical and psychosocial problems, for the patient	Items identified from three studies – cancer patients undergoing chemotherapy or follow-up with early disease; cancer patients undergoing chemotherapy for advanced ovarian cancer; cancer patients who were disease free	Used widely. Different formats available. Shown to be valid and reliable. Assessments are completed by patients – therefore evidence of missing data in one half or more in patients close to death
Hebrew Rehabilitation Centre for Ageing – Quality of Life index (HRCA–QL)[107,108]	Five items covering: health, support, outlook, daily living and mobility	Adapted from a quality of life index developed by Spitzer – the item mobility replaced one called activity. Items were identified by consensus of patients, the general public and professionals and aimed to apply to patients with all stages of disease	Used in the largest US evaluation of hospice care – the US National Hospice Study. Designed for completion by professionals, although has been completed by patients. The original Spitzer's index was validated, but the adapted index was not revalidated. Criticized for a lack of responsiveness in patients with advanced disease
The Support Team Assessment Schedule (STAS)[32,178,179]	17 items covering: pain and symptoms, psychosocial, insight, family needs, planning affairs, communication, home services and support of other professionals	Collaboration with five palliative support teams and revised in light of presentations at professional meetings, observation of palliative care, interviews with patients and families. Now used in different settings	Used widely. Time to complete on one patient averages two minutes. Validated to ensure professional ratings reflect patient views. Reliable. Reliance on professionals' assessments may be a problem but, where possible, has been tested with patients completing the assessments directly. Testing use of individual items, expanding symptom assessment and database under way
Edmonton Symptom Assessment System[180]	Nine visual analogue scales: pain, activity, nausea, depression, anxiety, drowsiness, appetite, well-being, shortness of breath	By members of hospice service	Inpatient hospice. In use and being validated

Continued

Table 11: *Continued*

Name and source	Number of items and domains included	How developed and setting	Comments on use
European Organisation for Research and Treatment of Cancer QLQ–C30[182]	30 items – multi-items and single scales	International collaboration of professionals – to devise items and scales. Measure tested in the different countries. Tested before and during chemotherapy in lung cancer patients	Being tested widely, in settings other than where originally developed. Patient completed – 11 minutes to complete. Shown to distinguish between patients at different stages of disease and valid, and reliable in those settings originally developed
Palliative Care Core Standards[184]	Six standard statements and 56 process and outcome items: collaboration with other agencies, symptom control, patient/carer information, emotional support, bereavement care and support, specialist education/training	Regional collaboration of hospice and home care units	Standards and measures developed and planning a pilot audit study to evaluate and review the core standards and to determine the criteria for the standards usage
		Inpatient hospice and community teams	
Regional study of care of the dying[37-40,171]	Questionnaire administered to the person who knows most about the patient, approximately seven months after their death. It assesses services received, symptoms during the last year of life, communication, satisfaction with care and mental status of the carer	Adapted from studies by Cartwright in 1967 and Cartwright and Seale in 1987	It builds on information collected 20 years ago and five years ago, so that patterns of care and symptoms can be compared
			The new study has interviewed the carers of 3500 people who died in 20 districts in England
Short Form-36 (SF-36)[185,186]	36 items assessing bodily pain, self-reported general health, mental health, limitations, energy, social functioning, change in health in last year (this last item is not a core domain and the time period can vary)	Is one of several health status questionnaires developed in the US by the Medical Outcomes Study (MOS). This is a 36-item short form of a longer questionnaire. Developed to assess the outcomes of hospital care in the US. Designed for patients at all stages of disease – from completely well to those with symptoms	Becoming very widely used. English (not American) version now available. Very quick to complete – a few minutes. This is its main advantage over other general (generic) measures such as the Nottingham Health Profile. The validity, reliability and responsiveness are often well regarded but the measure is undergoing further testing. Not yet tested in patients with advanced disease but has been tested in elderly patients and seems to be of most use to assess populations. Caution urged when trying to assess therapies or services

Continued

Table 11: *Continued*

Name and source	Number of items and domains included	How developed and setting	Comments on use
Hospital Anxiety and Depression scale (HAD)[41,183]	14 items – divided into two subscales; seven items to assess anxiety and seven to assess depression	Developed for patient completion in sick populations, translated into several languages. Validated against other scales	Described as quick and easy to use. Used widely in cancer patients, but its use in palliative care is still being tested
Karnofsky index[187]	Single item of mobility and functioning rated 0–100	Developed for completion by professional to assess chemotherapy	Limited because it only assesses functioning. Widely used in clinical records to give a quick indication of how sick a patient is. Shortened version – scored 0–5 – is available as European alternative
McGill pain questionnaire[188]	Pain is assessed by the patient ratings of the severity of a series of descriptors (e.g. throbbing)	Developed for completion by patients. At least five versions of the index are available – ranging from short form (15 descriptors) to longest version (128 descriptors)	Assesses only pain, not other aspects. Self-completion and verbal versions are available, although the originator recommended the verbal form. Good test–retest reliability
Standards of care for palliative nursing[125]	Seven topics – symptom control, spiritual support, family care, multi-professional team, ethical practice and staff support, each with structure, process and outcome criteria	Developed by a working group of the Royal College of Nursing which included five senior nurses for various settings. Standards follow the principles of the Dynamic Standard Setting System. Designed for a wide range of settings	This is the second revision of an earlier document. Standards can be adapted for local use. Like the Palliative Care Core Standards outcome criteria are given, but not ways to measure these. Such measures would need to be developed

Note: Other measures are available. See refs[173,189,190] for reviews of measures in palliative care and/or cancer care and refs[174,191–194] for reviews of measures in general.

Baseline data, to enable the monitoring of these targets, are usually lacking. The most important targets, e.g. controlling pain and symptoms or meeting communication needs, are the most difficult to monitor. However baselines could be established locally, through audit and outcomes projects and then monitored. Information on place of death is available routinely and this can be monitored. Note however that there is evidence that place of death is associated by social factors such as deprivation: in underprivileged areas fewer patients die at home compared with areas of higher privilege.[145] Therefore any targets which were monitored would need careful interpretation.

Service targets

More detailed examples of service targets can be found in the example service specification (Appendix VII). However targets for services could be as follow.

- To ensure that clinicians communicate effectively with patients, families and colleagues in relation to:
  a) pain and symptoms
  b) treatment regimens
  c) diagnosis
  d) follow-up and arrangements for care
  e) services available
  f) psychosocial problems and care available.
- To ensure that clinical protocols are developed, applied and audited in the management of patients with advanced progressive disease, including the use of therapies and mechanisms for referral for specialist advice.
- To ensure that health care professionals undertake and apply basic training in palliative care.
- That there is a multi-professional approach among specialist palliative care services.
- That services provide care suited to patients' individual cultural and ethnic needs. (Note there is evidence that the needs of patients from different ethnic groups may differ.[187,188,195,196]) Patients and families experience a range of emotional stages.[197]
- That non-cancer patients to be accepted by specialist palliative care services.

Process targets

- Full awareness among all GPs and relevant hospital staff of how to refer to palliative care services, and knowledge of the services available.[i]
- Increase in the proportion of appropriately timed referrals for specialist palliative care.
- Increase in the proportion of patients being cared for at home and dying at home.

These targets may be monitored through the service specifications or clinical audit, providing that clinicians as well as managers are fully signed up to them.

10 Research and information priorities

Priorities for further research

Main priorities, where research information is lacking, are as follow.

- Comparison of models of care, including different models of specialist palliative care, to determine:
  a) the most effective and cost-effective structure and process of care
  b) at what stage and for which patients and families specialist care is most effective.
- Evaluation of hospice at home and day care in terms of impact and cost-effectiveness.
- Evaluation of models of palliative care and treatment for non-cancer patients in terms of impact and cost-effectiveness.
- Comparison of different potential outcome measures of palliative care, in terms of their validity, reliability, responsiveness to clinical change, appropriateness and cost implications of their use.
- Evaluation of palliative care services for children and their families.
- Assessment of the needs of people from different backgrounds, cultural situations and ethnic groups.

Evaluations should ensure that appropriate outcome measures are used to assess effectiveness. Cost-effectiveness studies are particularly needed. Past studies have been criticized for weaknesses in these areas.[2,198]

Information priorities

- Nationally, for OPCS – the recording of hospice as a place of death should be included as a separate category. Coders could be provided with details and listings, for example from the St Christopher's Hospice Directory. This would allow study of the trends of hospice as a place of death.
- Nationally, trends in place of death should be monitored.
- For purchasers – as much as possible, purchasers should agree the details and coding of information required from specialist palliative services, to ensure that data can be aggregated at regional or national levels. Ideally, a core minimum data set should be agreed. One is currently being piloted by the National Council for Hospice and Specialist Palliative Care Services.
- For providers – standardized data collection should be used which includes demographic details including ethnic group, place of care, diagnosis, problems or symptom profile, and outcomes. Examples of such systems are available.[199-201] Coding systems should be compatible with the NHS and include the NHS number.
- For providers – details of service costs are needed.

Appendix I Purchasing specialist palliative care services 1994/95

Allocations

The allocation of funds to each region for 1994/95 is based on the estimated distribution of population in the 65–84 age group as follows.

Region	Amount in £000s
Northern	2308
Yorkshire	2710
Trent	3498
East Anglian	1679
North West Thames	2358
North East Thames	2624
South East Thames	2906
South West Thames	2304
Wessex	2426
Oxford	1646
South Western	2805
West Midlands	3772
Mersey	1747
North Western	2917
Total	**35700**

Source: EL(94)14 Annex A[15]

Appendix II Specialist palliative care services (adapted from information for purchasers: background to available specialist palliative care services[24])

Community services in patients' own homes

Specialist service	Availability[a]	Nature/role
Home care team from local IP unit[b]	Widely available 100+ in UK	Generally work in conjunction with primary care team. Advise on symptom control and availability and relevance of other services. Often have direct access to other specialist palliative care services and round-the-clock nursing services
Macmillan community-based free-standing team	200+ in UK	
Hospice at home staff clinical nurse specialist – hospital or community-based	Not known	
Marie Curie nursing service	Over 5000 'bank' nurses available in almost all areas	Hands-on nursing around the clock. Accessed via district nurse or Macmillan nurse. Increasingly organized by Marie Curie Cancer Care regional nurse manager[b]
Rapid response teams home respite care hospice at home services (some)	Limited availability as yet but developing	These services are multi-disciplinary and are provided on a 24-hour basis to avoid admission where this would otherwise be necessary and/or to fill in gaps until other services come into play. Apart from hospice at home services, these are additional responsibilities being developed by inpatient units
Specialist medical service	Widely available	Telephone advisory service generally provided by all inpatient Specialist Palliative Care Units (SPCUs) and multi-disciplinary teams. Visits to patients made by arrangement with GP. Not limited to cancer
Social work physiotherapy occupational therapy	Limited service given by same SPCUs	May be available to work with patients direct or advise the primary care team on patients referred and accepted by the specialist palliative care unit
Bereavement services	Widely available but generally limited to families/friends of patients cared for by the SPCU	Increasingly part of services offered by SPCUs through trained staff (often volunteers)

[a] Figures in column 2 are drawn from the 1995 *Directory of Hospice and Palliative Care Services.*
[b] Historical focus on cancer (not Sue Ryder) but patients with other diagnoses are increasingly accepted.

Institution-based services for patients not requiring admission or after discharge

Service	Availability[a]	Nature/role
Day care free-standing or attached to a specialist palliative care unit	Widely available. 220 units providing day care	Accent on rehabilitation and independence. A variety of services offered, e.g. physio/OT/aromatherapy, as well as nursing and medical care, if appropriate
Outpatient clinics	Often offered by specialist palliative care inpatient units	Medical or other specialist service, e.g. lymphoedema, available through referral from GP or hospital doctor

Inpatient facilities

Service	Availability[a]	Nature/role
NHS specialist palliative care units voluntary/hospice[b] (Marie Curie/Sue Ryder and many others)	2500+ beds (England and Wales)	Specialist inpatient care with accent on symptom control, support for families, etc.
Hospital palliative care/support team or nurse	200+ (England and Wales)	Teams, increasingly multi-disciplinary, working in an advisory capacity in a hospital setting. Not limited to either cancer or patients with very late stage disease
Hospital clinical nurse specialists or physicians (some Macmillan)	Increasing	Individuals with palliative remit, usually based on oncology departments
Hospital physicians in palliative medicine	Increasing	Consultants in the specialty, not necessarily with associated teams and often based in a local SPCU, but with committed sessions for advising colleagues and treating patients by arrangement

[a] Figures in column 2 drawn from the 1995 *Directory of Hospice and Palliative Care Services*.
[b] Historical focus on cancer (not Sue Ryder) but patients with other diagnoses are increasingly accepted.

Appendix III Standardized mortality ratios for selected causes, all ages (1990–94); example

		1990/94 Standardized mortality ratio
All malignant neoplasms (ICD 140–208)	Men	100
	Women	140
	Total	102
Malignant neoplasm of trachea, bronchus and lung (ICD 162)	Men	103
	Women	142
	Total	115
Malignant neoplasm of:		
female breast (ICD 174)	Women	93
cervix uteri (ICD 410–414)	Women	105
Ischaemic heart disease (ICD 430–438)	Men	81
	Women	72
	Total	77
Cerebrovascular disease (ICD 430–414)	Men	79
	Women	62
	Total	68
Motor vehicle traffic accidents (ICD E810–819)	Men	68
	Women	87
	Total	74
Suicide and self-inflicted injury and injury undetermined (ICD E950–959, E980–989)	Men	190
	Women	248
	Total	208
Suicide and self-inflicted injury (ICD E950–959)	Men	142
	Women	273
	Total	179
All above causes (except all malignant neoplasms)	Men	87
	Women	78
	Total	83
All causes (all ages) (ICD 001–999)	Men	100
	Women	87
	Total	93

Note: ICD 9 coding used.

Appendix IV An example of the results of analysis of characteristics of patients who may need palliative care for the district of Kensington, Chelsea and Westminster (KCW)[a]

Analysis of place and cause of death in KCW (1988–92)

To consider the palliative care for patients within KCW in more detail, place of death has been analysed separately for people dying from cancer, circulatory diseases and other disease. The following have been examined:

- the trends in place of death over the five years
- place of death by ward (using all the five years data combined, to avoid very small numbers).

The sample (five years in KCW)

The sample consists of 15 805 deaths registered between 1988 and 1992 inclusive. This accounts for all the deaths of residents of KCW.

There were 6481 deaths within Kensington & Chelsea and 9324 deaths within Westminster (Table A1).

Table A1: Number of deaths in KCW: 1988–92

Borough	n	%
Kensington & Chelsea	6481	41.0
Westminster	9324	59.0
Total	15805	100.0

There were approximately equal numbers of men and women who died and the rate was constant over the years (Tables A2, A3). (Note: a few deaths in 1987 are included in this sample because of the delay in registering. Similarly a few deaths in 1992 will not be recorded until 1993.)

Table A2: Sex of deaths in KCW: 1988–92

Sex	n	%
Men	7945	50.3
Women	7860	49.7
Total	15805	100.0

---

[a]Source: Higginson et al.[158]

Table A3: Year of death in KCW sample

Year	n	%
1987	64	0.4
1988	3281	20.8
1989	3342	21.1
1990	3066	19.4
1991	3150	19.9
1992	2902	18.4
Total	15805	100.0

The majority of patients who died were elderly (Table A4).

Table A4: Number of deaths by age in KCW: 1988–92

Age (years)	n	%
<15	129	0.8
16–35	508	3.2
36–64	2942	18.6
65–74	3389	21.4
75+	8837	55.9
Total	15805	100.0

Cause of death (five years in KCW)

The most common causes of death were diseases of the circulatory system, neoplasms or diseases of the respiratory system. Table A5 shows the number of people who died from these diseases and other diseases, which may potentially have a terminal period, such as dementia, liver cirrhosis. etc. There were 2213 (14%) deaths which were unlikely to have had a terminal period.

Table A5: Cause of death in KCW: 1988–92

Disease recorded on death certificate	n	%
Neoplasms (cancers)	4171	26.4
Nutritional and metabolic	326	2.1
Dementia	122	0.8
Nervous system	296	1.9
Circulatory system	6316	40.0
Respiratory system	2015	12.7
Liver cirrhosis	225	1.4
Musculo–skeletal system	121	0.8
Other diseases, not at all likely to have a terminal/palliative period	2213	14.0
Total	15805	100.0

Place of death (five years in KCW)

The majority of deaths occurred in hospital (69%) and 24% occurred at home (Table A6).

Table A6: Place of death in KCW: 1988–92

Place	n	%
NHS non-psychiatric hospital	9524	60.3
Non-NHS psychiatric hospital	2	0.0
NHS psychiatric hospital	22	0.1
Private hospital	1316	8.3
Other communal establishment	679	4.3
At home	3735	23.6
Elsewhere	527	3.3
Total	15805	100.0

Analysis of place of death by cause, borough and ward: 1988–92

The percentage of patients who died at home and in hospital have been analysed for those who died from neoplasms, circulatory diseases and other potentially terminal conditions for the years from 1988 to 1992. The 2213 cases unlikely to have had a terminal period have been excluded from this analysis.

Deaths due to neoplasms

Examination of trends over the years suggests a slight increase in the percentage of patients dying at home from neoplasms within Kensington & Chelsea. There may be also a slight increase within the City of Westminster, although there appears to have been a fall between 1991 and 1992 (Figures A1–A3).

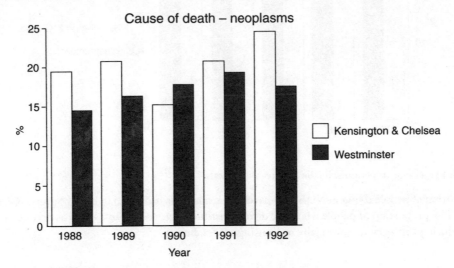

Figure A1: Percentage of people who die at home.

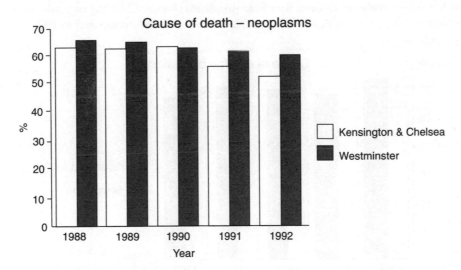

Figure A2: Percentage of people who die in NHS non-psychiatric hospitals.

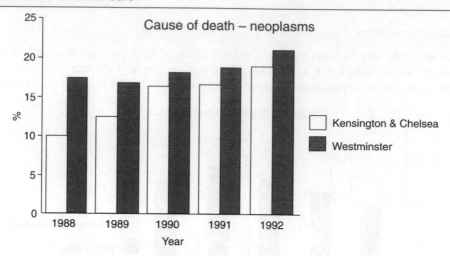

Figure A3: Percentage of people who die in private hospitals.

The proportion of people dying in NHS non-psychiatric hospitals has fallen in both boroughs between 1988 and 1992. The proportion of people who have died in institutions recorded by OPCS as private hospitals has increased during this period – especially in Kensington & Chelsea.

Circulatory diseases

The proportion of people who died in each setting from circulatory diseases is largely unchanged over these years – there appears to be a slight reduction in home deaths. However in general there is a higher proportion of deaths at home for circulatory diseases than from neoplasms (Figures A4–A6) especially in Westminster. In this borough in 1992, 17% of deaths from neoplasms died at home, compared to 29% of deaths from circulatory diseases.

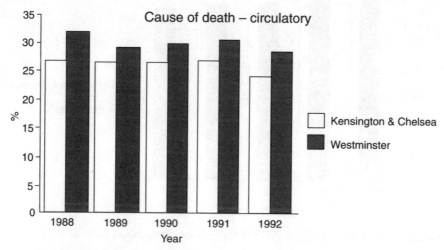

Figure A4: Percentage of people who die at home.

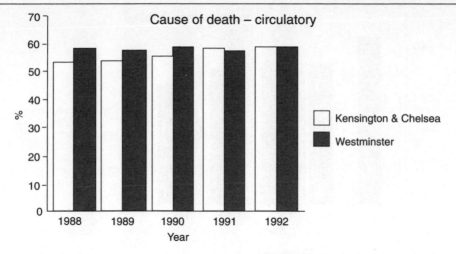

Figure A5: Percentage of people who die in non-psychiatric hospitals.

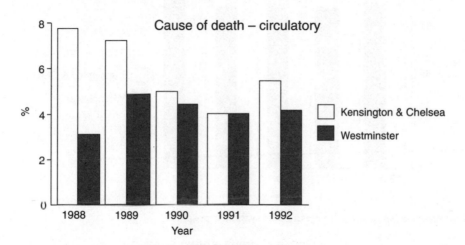

Figure A6: Percentage of people who die in private hospitals.

Other terminal diseases

There appears to be no trend over the years for people who have died of other terminal diseases, apart from a suggestion of an increased use of private hospitals (Figures A7–A9).

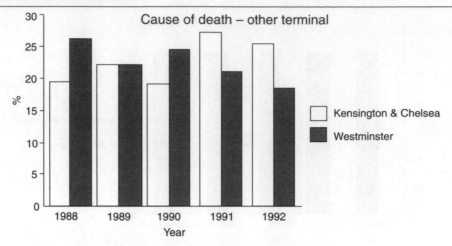

Figure A7: Percentage of people who die at home.

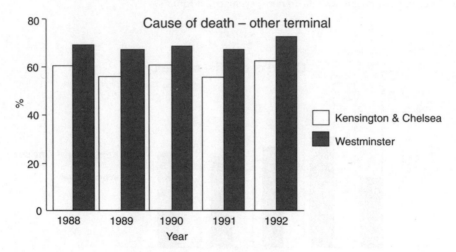

Figure A8: Percentage of people who die in non-psychiatric hospitals.

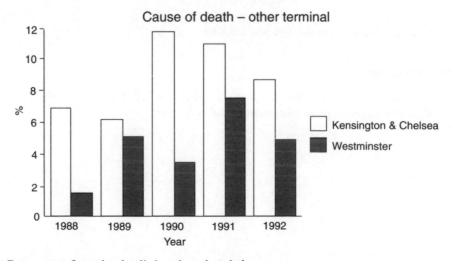

Figure A9: Percentage of people who die in private hospitals.

All data combined for neoplasms, circulatory and other terminal diseases

Figures A10 to A12 show the percentage of people who died from all the aforementioned diseases. The only apparent trend is an increase in the use of private hospitals, as was found separately for neoplasms.

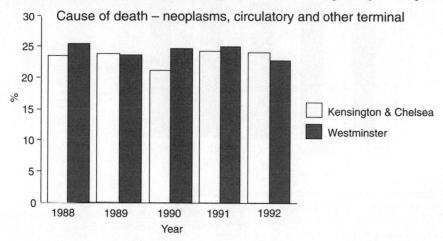

Figure A10: Percentage of people who die at home.

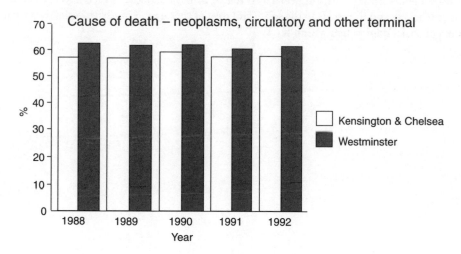

Figure A11: Percentage of people who die in non-psychiatric hospitals.

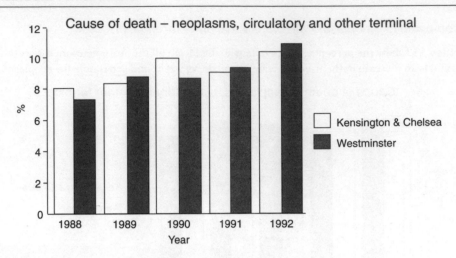

Figure A12: Percentage of people who die in private hospitals.

Analysis of data by ward

Figures A13 to A16 show the proportions of deaths occurring at home for the different wards during the five-year period for patients who died from neoplasms, circulatory diseases, other terminal diseases and these catagories combined. Certain wards appear consistently to have a higher percentage of deaths at home, notably Knightsbridge and the wards to the south and west of this area. This distribution is similar to that of the indicators of social deprivation within KCW.[202]

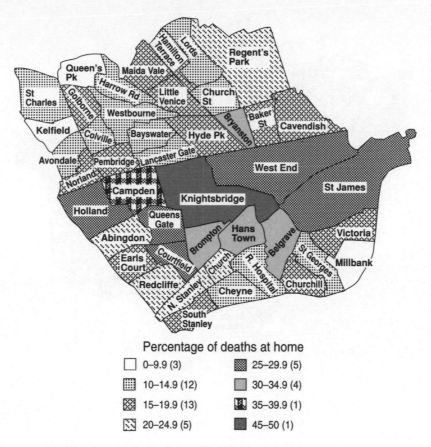

Figure A13: Percentage of deaths at home by electoral ward: neoplasms.

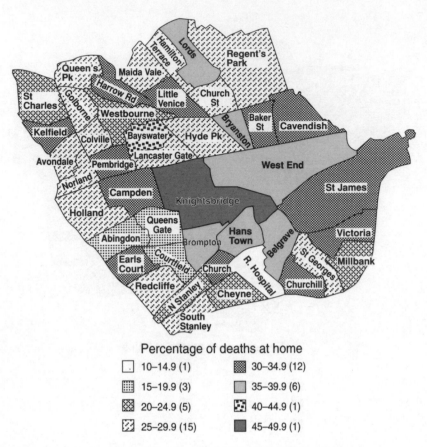

Percentage of deaths at home

- [.] 10–14.9 (1)
- 15–19.9 (3)
- 20–24.9 (5)
- 25–29.9 (15)
- 30–34.9 (12)
- 35–39.9 (6)
- 40–44.9 (1)
- 45–49.9 (1)

Figure A14: Percentage of deaths at home by electoral ward: circulatory disorders.

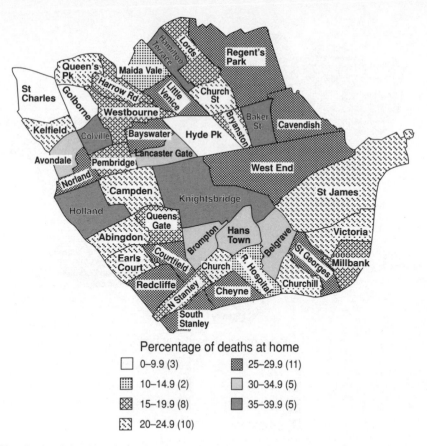

Percentage of deaths at home

□	0–9.9 (3)	▨	25–29.9 (11)
▦	10–14.9 (2)	▨	30–34.9 (5)
▨	15–19.9 (8)	▨	35–39.9 (5)
▨	20–24.9 (10)		

Figure A15: Percentage of deaths at home by electoral ward: other diseases with a terminal period.

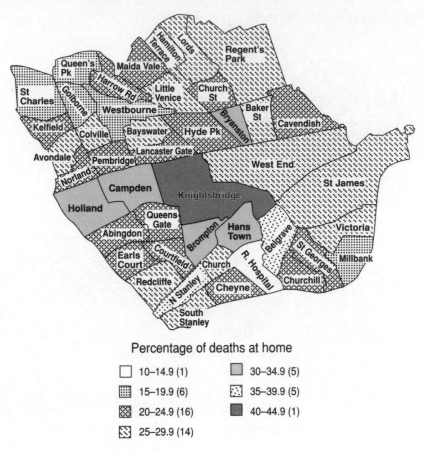

Percentage of deaths at home

☐ 10–14.9 (1)   ▨ 30–34.9 (5)

▦ 15–19.9 (6)   ⦙ 35–39.9 (5)

▩ 20–24.9 (16)   ■ 40–44.9 (1)

▧ 25–29.9 (14)

Figure A16: Percentage of deaths at home by electoral ward: neoplasms, circulatory and other terminal disorders combined.

Appendix V Growth in palliative care in UK and Ireland: 1965–95

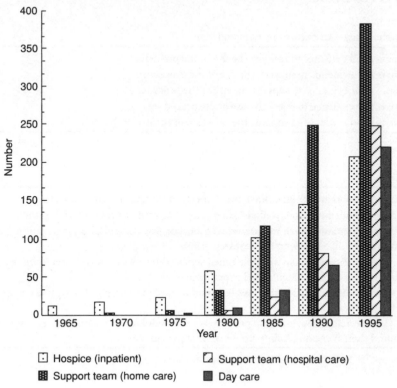

Key:

Hospice (inpatient)　　Support team (hospital care)

Support team (home care)　　Day care

Appendix VI Grades for assessment of quality of scientific evidence

Analysis of service efficacy – strength of recommendation

A	There is good evidence to support the use of the procedure
B	There is fair evidence to support the use of the procedure
C	There is poor evidence to support the use of the procedure
D	There is fair evidence to reject the use of the procedure
E	There is good evidence to support the rejection of the use of the procedure

Source: Stevens and Raftery (1994)[21]

Quality of the evidence

(I)	Evidence obtained from at least one properly randomized controlled trial
(II-1)	Evidence obtained from well designed controlled trials without randomization
(II-2)	Evidence obtained from well designed cohort or case controlled analytic studies, preferably from more than one centre or research group
(II-3)	Evidence obtained from multiple timed series with or without the interventions, or from dramatic results in uncontrolled experiments
(III)	Opinions of respected authorities based on clinical experience, descriptive studies or reports of expert committees
(IV)	Evidence inadequate owing to problems of methodology, e.g. sample size, length or comprehensiveness of follow-up, or conflict in evidence

Table adapted from US Task Force on Preventive Health Care.
Source: Stevens and Raftery (1994)[21]

Appendix VII Kensington & Chelsea and Westminster Health Authority service specification: palliative care services

Introduction

Kensington & Chelsea and Westminster Health Authority (KCWHA) has recently undertaken a detailed and in-depth review of specialist palliative care services. Following the production of a report and a seminar with all major providers of palliative care services, this service specification outlines KCW's requirements for palliative care services.[a]

The specification relates to all services apart from paediatric and HIV palliative care services. (There is currently a separate specification for HIV services but we would aim to integrate both these specifications in the future.)

For the purposes of this specification the following UK definition of palliative care has been adopted.

Palliative care is active total care offered to a patient with a progressive illness and their family when it is recognised that the illness is no longer curable, in order to concentrate on the quality of life and the alleviation of distressing symptoms within the framework of a co-ordinated service. Palliative care neither hastens nor postpones death, it provides a relief from pain and other distressing symptoms, integrates the psychological and spiritual aspects of care. In addition it offers a support system to help during the patient's illness and in bereavement. 'Family' is used as a general term to cover closely attached individuals, whatever their legal status. (Standing Medical Advisory Committee and Standing Nursing and Midwifery Advisory Committee 1992.)

Strategic principles

KCWHA wishes to incorporate the following principles into the palliative care services it commissions.

- To ensure the authority commissions a comprehensive range of specialist palliative care services which are of high quality and cost-effective.
- To secure equity of access to these services for differing groups of diagnoses, by ensuring services are appropriate to the specific needs of KCW residents and that details of services available are widely known, particularly with regard to how to refer into the service.
- To commission services which will allow patients and their carers choice of care models, in particular ensuring that patients can remain within their own home settings for as long as they may wish.
- To ensure that service provision to patients and their carers is seamless even if the care is being shared between a range of different providers, including other social services, housing and voluntary providers.
- To ensure that all health staff involved in direct patient and family care are well versed in good practice principles of palliative care.
- To ensure that services commissioned are of the highest quality standards and that these standards are regularly monitored.
- To ensure that service providers are regularly involved in clinical audit and measurement of effectiveness of outcomes of interventions, which will be jointly agreed with purchasers.

---

[a] Copies of the report are available from the authority and contain a reference list.

Context

Considerable changes are currently taking place within specialist palliative care services, which have caused some uncertainty particularly to voluntary hospice providers; these are as follow.

- Monies previously ring-fenced specifically for voluntary hospices have now been devolved from regional health authorities to districts and can now be used for any specialist palliative care services.
- 1994 sees voluntary hospice providers for the first time having to come into the market and set contracts with health authorities. This has involved the setting of agreed levels of activity and finance and setting clearer criteria for admission. Service developments now must be agreed with purchasers in advance.
- There has been an increase in the number of hospice providers within greater London, which has caused current providers concerns as to their viability with increased competition.
- A growing awareness of an inequity in access to palliative care services for non-cancer patients.
- The Calman report on cancer services suggesting a reduction in the number of treatment centres providing specialist care within acute hospitals will influence the distribution of services locally.

Population/health needs

Kensington, Chelsea and Westminster covers an area of 13 square miles in North West London and is coterminous with its two constituent local authorities. According to the OPCS mid-1991 population estimates, the resident population of the district is 323 900 (141 400 in the Royal Borough of Kensington & Chelsea and 182 500 in the City of Westminster).

The population is an inner-city population and includes people from a range of different cultural and ethnic groups. There is a wide range of health experiences across the different wards within the area. The most disadvantaged wards display higher rates of death and increased levels of illness, high levels of unemployment and poorer housing, with many single parent families and elderly people who live alone.

Analysis of potential needs for palliative care showed that 830 KCW residents die from cancer each year. The majority of these are aged over 75 years. National statistics suggest that of these almost 700 would experience pain in the last year of life, almost 400 would have trouble with breathing and 400 would have symptoms of vomiting or nausea. Many would have other symptoms. KCW residents who die from other causes were also considered, such as circulatory diseases, which may have a palliative period. Each year approximately 1700 KCW residents die from these diseases, as for cancer the majority are elderly. National statistics would suggest that of these almost 1200 would experience pain in the last year of life, 850 would experience trouble with breathing and 450 would have symptoms of vomiting or nausea. Again many had other symptoms or a combination of symptoms.

Patients will also need emotional, spiritual and social support. Many of the families of these patients would require support during care and in bereavement.

Within KCW approximately 24% of deaths occur at home and 69% occur in hospital. For cancer patients an even smaller proportion – 18% – die at home. The percentage of patients who die at home varies greatly across KCW ranging from less than 10% in some of our electoral wards to greater than 40% in others. The distribution appears to mirror that of the Jarman indicators for social deprivation within KCW.

Examining trends over the years indicates that there has been a slight increase in the percentage of cancer patients who die at home in the Royal Borough of Kensington & Chelsea but probably not in the City of Westminster. There was also a fall in the proportion of people who died in NHS hospitals and an increase in the proportion who died in private hospitals.

Preferred model of service

In the review KCW identified current service provision and the report and the seminar highlighted areas where service changes were required. From specialist providers KCW will wish to commission a package of care which will range through symptom control, psychological support for the patient and the carers, respite care within the community, terminal care and bereavement care. Other providers will assist in the provision of a seamless, comprehensive service to the patient and their carers.

The main recommendations in response to the concerns raised in the KCW review report were as follow.

- Links between Macmillan and support nurses working in acute hospitals and the hospices and specialist palliative care teams needed to be more formalized.
- There was a need to cascade support from the specialist services through into generic services, perhaps in the form of in-reach teams into acute hospitals.
- There needed to be more accurate reporting of activity, particularly the activity of the Macmillan nurses in the Chelsea and Westminster Hospital should be clearly indentified for purchasers.
- For data collection there needed to be greater clarity in the requirements and reasons for process data. This would ensure that personnel could improve the quality of their data collection.
- Data collection was also needed on the outcomes and quality of care given, for example symptom control, safe discharge and appropriateness of interventions.
- Links between acute providers and hospices needed to be formalized.
- Similarly links between hospices and specialist palliative care services and primary care staff needed to be improved.
- GPs required better information on the services available, but rather than have this in the form of directories it was suggested that the KCW 'place mats' would be a useful approach. Advertising information was not felt to be helpful.
- There was a need to develop patient agreements or protocols between services to ensure that duplication did not occur but that good liaison did.
- A 24-hour service provision was thought to be essential for home care in collaboration with appropriate social services.
- GPs should be made aware of those services which provide 24-hour advice and support and where patients in the care of a service or already known to a hospice may be admitted out of hours as an emergency.
- Greater investigation of the access to services for people from black and ethnic minority groups was needed and in particular KCW needs to determine how many patients from this group are likely to need palliative care services and what their preferences may be.
- Work is also needed to determine the language needs of people from ethnic groups and the availability of translators for patients who are cared for at home.
- Training is needed for generic workers to ensure that all staff are aware of good practice in palliative care.
- There was a general need to be mature about interprofessional working relationships.

Attached to this service specification is a range of standards which outline the preferred model of services that KCW wishes to commission.

Although all standards are not appropriate to all providers it is essential to note that patients will move between the varying providers and their care must be a continuum so that all services are linked.

These standards cover general quality requirements, data requirements and clinical audit. It should be noted that it is not anticipated that all standards will be regularly monitored. An initial position statement from each provider will be prepared and agreement reached between the provider and KCW as to which specific standards will be monitored in any one year.

Monitoring

KCW places great emphasis on information and the monitoring of not only activity, but of the quality of the service commissioned and the agreed outcome. It is anticipated that reporting on achievement of specific quality standards as outlined in this specification will be incorporated into schedule 4 of KCW contracts and will therefore be monitored on a twice-yearly basis.

Audit and outcome

Arrangements for clinical audit and development of outcome measures

- An audit is requested of the treatment and management of symptoms of pain, anxiety and family problems using or adapting already established outcomes tools such as the Support Team Assessment Schedule (STAS). Providers are requested to present results of this to purchasers and to demonstrate what action they are intending to take as a result of any problems found with the services.
- Providers are requested to demonstrate and to audit joint initiatives with local practitioners and primary care teams or acute hospitals in enhancing the quality of care offered to terminally ill patients and in particular including those who do not have cancer and their families or carers.

To commission a comprehensive range of palliative care services

Standard	Ability to comply	Monitoring mechanism
Specialist palliative care providers will provide packages of care that will include:		
• Inpatient care		
a) symptom control		
b) psychological support		
c) respite care		
d) terminal care		
• Day care – at current levels only until evaluation has been undertaken		
• Care within the community		
a) symptom control		
b) psychological support		
c) maintenance		
d) terminal care		
• Bereavement and after-care services		
Pain control		
• Patients will have access to specialist pain control advice which complies with agreed clinical guidelines		
Emotional support		
• Emotional support will be available to the patient and their carer by staff with an understanding of/or training in general counselling techniques. Specialist counselling advice will be available from suitably trained personnel when appropriate		

Continued

To commission a comprehensive range of palliative care services: *continued*

Standard	Ability to comply	Monitoring mechanism
• Bereavement after-care services will be available to relatives and carers, linking with voluntary services where appropriate		

Co-ordination
- Patients should have access to a range of professionals with specialist palliative care skills
- Where the multi-disciplinary team is not centrally managed, formal interprofessional working arrangements should be in place, with a designated head of service, which includes medical care
- Specialist palliative care nurses and multi-disciplinary teams should have formal working agreements with a hospice with whom KCW holds a contract
- Recognized complementary therapies, which are known to be clinically effective should be available to patients where appropriate
- Link nurses (in addition to specialist palliative care nurses) should be identified within the community and on hospital wards to act as a resource on palliative care services
- Prior to discharge from inpatient care there will be a clear mechanism for co-ordination of care on discharge with named lead care provider

To secure equity of access to services by ensuring they are appropriate to the specific needs of KCW residents

Standard	Ability to comply	Monitoring mechanism

Availability
- Urgent referrals can be made to the service seven days a week
- Specialist providers will offer a single contact number for GPs and hospitals to obtain advice about a patient

Cultural beliefs
- Provision should be made to allow patients to observe their own faith (or non-faith) and facilitate their spiritual leaders to enter the hospice
- Providers will not impose their personal religious beliefs on patients unless the patient initiates/requests support
- Cultural beliefs about death and dying will be properly observed
- Meals should meet cultural and religious requirements
- Patients and their carers should have access to interpreting advocacy services where necessary

References

1 Working Group on Terminal Care (chairman: E Wilkes). National terminal care policy. *J Roy Coll Gen Practit* 1980; **30**: 466–71.

2 Higginson I. Palliative Care: a review of past challenges and future trends. *J Public Hlth* 1993; **15(1)**: 3–8.

3 Saunders C, Sykes N. *The management of terminal malignant disease*. 3rd edn. London: Edward Arnold, 1993.

4 Standing Medical Advisory Committee and Standing Nurse and Midwifery Advisory Committee. *The Principles and Provision of Palliative Care*. London: Joint Report of the Standing Medical Advisory Committee & Standing Nurse & Midwifery Advisory Committee, 1992.

5 Marie Curie Memorial Foundation. *The Marie Curie Memorial Foundation; a brief history 1948–1984*. London: Marie Curie Memorial Foundation, 28 Belgrave Square, 1985.

6 Lunt BJ, Hillier ER. Terminal care: present services and future priorities. *Br Med J* 1981; **283**: 595–8.

7 Lunt B. Terminal cancer care services: recent changes in regional inequalities in Great Britain. *Soc Sci Med* 1987; **20(7)**: 753–9.

8 Cartwright A. Changes in life and care in the year before death 1969–1987. *J Pub Hlth Med* 1991; **13(2)**: 81–7.

9 Office of Population Censuses and Surveys. Mortality statistics general. Series DH1 No. 26 Review of the Registrar General on deaths in England and Wales, 1992. London: HMSO, 1994.

10 Bowling A. The hospitalisation of death: should more people die at home? *J Med Ethics* 1983; **9**: 158–61.

11 Department of Health. London: DoH Circular HC(87)4(2).

12 Department of Health. Press release. *Extra £8 million Government money for hospices*. London: Department of Health Press Office, 1989: 89/556.

13 Department of Health. Press release. *Government gives £17 million more for hospices*. London: Department of Health Press Office, 1991: H91/6.

14 Department of Health. Press release. *£37 million more for hospices*. London, Department of Health Press Office, 1992: H92/96.

15 NHS Management Executive. Contracting for specialist palliative care services. NHS Management Executive 1994: EL(94)14.

16 NHS Executive. Specialist palliative care services including Drugs for Hospices scheme. NHS Executive 1995: EL(95)22.

17 1995 Director of Hospice Services in the UK and the Republic of Ireland. St Christopher's Hospice Information Service. London: St Christopher's Hospice, Sydenham, 1995.

18 Heginbotham C. Rationing. *Br Med J* 1992; **304**: 496–9.

19 Department of Public Health. *Health and Lifestyle Survey*. London: Department of Public Health, Kensington, Chelsea and Westminster Health Authority, 1994.

20 Caroll G. *Priorities for health care*. Essex: Department of Public Health, Essex Health Authority, 1992.

21 Stevens A, Raftery J. The epidemiological approach to needs assessment. In *Health Care Needs Assessment* (eds A Stevens, J Raftery). Oxford: Radcliffe Medical Press 1994; pp. 21–30 (volume 1).

22 National Council for Hospice and Specialist Palliative Care Services. *Specialist palliative care: a statement of definitions*. London: National Council for Hospice and Specialist Palliative Care Services, 1995.

23 WHO Expert Committee. *Cancer pain relief and palliative care*. No. 804. Geneva: World Health Organization Technical Report Series, 1990.

24 Working party on clinical guidelines in palliative care (drafted by G Ford). *Information for purchasers. Background to available specialist palliative care services*. London: National Council for Hospice and Specialist Palliative Care Services, 1995.

25 European Association for Palliative Care – European Association for Palliative Care Constitution, Milan 1988.

26 National Association of Health Authorities and Trusts. *Care of People with a Terminal Illness.* Birmingham Research Park, Vincent Drive, Birmingham B15 2SQ, 1991.

27 McCarthy M, Higginson IJ. Clinical audit by a palliative care team. *Palliative Medicine* 1991; **5(3)**: 215–21.

28 Office of Population Censuses and Surveys. *Population Trends 74*, Winter 1993. Tables 13 and 14. Deaths rates by age, sex and selected causes. London: HMSO, 1994.

29 Expert Advisory Group on Cancer to the Chief Medical Officers of England and Wales. A policy framework for commissioning cancer services. London: Department of Health, 1995.

30 NHS Executive. A policy framework for commissioning cancer services. NHS Executive 1995: EL(95)51.

31 Gau DW, Diehl AK. Disagreement among general practitioners regarding cause of death. *Br Med J* 1982; **284**: 239–445.

32 Higginson I, McCarthy M. Validity of the support team assessment schedule: do staffs' ratings reflect those made by patients or their families? *Palliat Med* 1993; **7**: 219–28.

33 Epstein AM, Hall JA, Tognetti J *et al.* Using proxies to evaluate quality of life. Can they provide valid information about patient's health status and satisfaction with medical care. *Medical Care* 1989; **27(3)**: S91–S98.

34 Field D, Douglas C, Jagger C *et al.* Terminal illness: views of patients and their lay carers. *Palliat Med* 1995; **9**: 45–54.

35 Higginson I, Priest P, McCarthy M. Are bereaved family members a valid proxy for a patient's assessment of dying? *Soc Sci Med* 1994; **38(4)**: 553–7.

36 Seale C. A comparison of hospice and conventional care. *Soc Sci Med* 1991; **32(2)**: 147–52.

37 Addington-Hall JM. *Regional study of care for the dying.* Feedback for district health authorities. Cancer deaths only. London: Department of Epidemiology and Public Health, University College London, 1993.

38 Addington-Hall JM. *Regional study of care for the dying.* Feedback for district health authorities. Non-cancer deaths only. London: Department of Epidemiology and Public Health, University College London, 1993.

39 Addington-Hall JM, McCarthy M. Regional study of care of the dying. methods and sample characteristics. *Palliat Med* 1995; **9**: 27–35.

40 Addington-Hall JM, McCarthy M. Dying from cancer: results of a national population-based investigation. *Palliat Med* 1995; **9**: 295–305.

41 Hopwood P, Howell A, Maguire P. Psychiatric morbidity in patients with advanced cancer of the breast: prevalence measured by two self-rating questionnaires. *Br J Cancer* 1991; **62(2)**: 349–52.

42 Bennett M, Corcoran G. The impact on community palliative care services of a hospital palliative care team. *Palliat Med* 1994; **8**: 237–44.

43 Higginson I, Wade A, McCarthy M. Effectiveness of two palliative support teams. *J Pub Hlth Med* 1992; **1**: 50–6.

44 Addington-Hall JM, MacDonald L, Anderson H *et al.* Dying from cancer: the view of bereaved family and the friends about the experiences of terminally ill patients. *Palliat Med* 1991; **5**: 207–14.

45 Eve A, Jackson A. Palliative care, where are we now? *Palliat Care Today* 1994; **1**: 22–3.

46 Frankel S. Assessing the need for hospice beds. *Hlth Trnd* 1990; **2**: 83–6.

47 Hockley JM, Dunlop R, Davis RJ. Survey of distressing symptoms in dying patients and their families in hospital and the response to a symptom control team. *Br Med J* 1988; **296**: 1715–7.

48 Severs MP, Wilkins PS. A hospital palliative care ward for elderly people. *Age and Ageing* 1991; **20(5)**: 361–4.

49 Noble B. A snapshot survey of hospital and hospice patients. In: *Older peoples: palliative care strategy*. Sheffield: Family and Community Services, Health Authority and Family Health Services Authority, 1993, Appendix B.

50 PHLS AIDS Centre – Communicable Disease Surveillance Centre and Scottish Centre for Infection and Environmental Health. Unpublished Quarterly Surveillance Tables No.25, December 1994 Tables 2 and 3a.

51 Butters E, Higginson I, Hearn J et al. *Prospective audit of community care for people with HIV/AIDS provided by health, social and voluntary sector teams*. Report to North Thames Region. London: London School of Hygiene and Tropical Medicine, 1995.

52 Moss V. Care for patients with advanced HIV and AIDS disease. *Palliat Care in Terminal Illness* 1994; **2**: 84–93.

53 Cole RM. Medical aspects of care for the person with advanced acquired immunodeficiency syndrome (AIDS): a palliative care perspective. *Palliat Med* 1991; **5**: 96–111.

54 Welch JM. Symptoms of HIV disease. *Palliat Med* 1991; **5**: 46–51.

55 Dixon P, Higginson I. AIDS and cancer pain treated with slow release morphine. *Postgrad Med J* 1991; **67** (Suppl. 2): S92–S94.

56 Butters E, Higginson I, George R et al. Assessing the symptoms, anxiety and practical needs of HIV/AIDS patients reviewing palliative care. *Quality of Life Research* 1992; **1**: 47–51.

57 Bulkin W, Brown L, Fraioli D et al. Hospice Care of the Intravenous Drug User AIDS Patient in a Skilled Nurse Facility. *J Acq Imm Def Synd* 1988; **1**: 375–80.

58 Rosci MA, Pigorini F, Bernabei A et al. Methods for detecting early signs of AIDS dementia complex in asymptomatic HIV-1-infected subjects. *AIDS* 1992; **6(11)**: 1309–16.

59 Bornstein RA, Nasrallah HA, Para MF et al. Neuropsychological performance in symptomatic and asymptomatic HIV infection. *AIDS* 1993; **7**: 519–24.

60 McKeogh M. Dementia in HIV disease: a challenge for palliative care. *J Palliat Care* 1995; **11(2)**: 30–3.

61 Higginson I, Mallandain I, Butters E et al. What services are needed to care for people with HIV/AIDS encephalopathy in North Thames. London: London School of Hygiene and Tropical Medicine, 1995.

62 *1994 Directory of Hospice Services in the UK and the Republic of Ireland*. St Christopher's Hospice Information Service. London: St Christopher's Hospice, Sydenham, 1994.

63 Crone S, Rigge M, Whalley P. *The Pain Clinic Directory 1994*. London: College of Health, 1994.

64 Doyle D, Hanks GWC, MacDonald N (eds). *Oxford Textbook of Palliative Medicine*. Oxford: Oxford University Press, 1993.

65 Twycross RG. Cancer pain a global perspective. The Edinburgh Symposium on Pain and Medical Education. In *Royal Society of Medicine International Symposium Series (149)* (RG Twycross ed.), London, 1989, pp. 3–16.

66 Larve F, Colleau SM, Brasseur L et al. Multicentre study of cancer pain and its treatment in France. *Br Med J* 1995; **310**: 1034–9.

67 Ventafridda V, Tamburini M, Caraceni C et al. A validation study of the WHO method for cancer pain relief. *Cancer* 1987; **59**: 850–6.

68 Working Party on Clinical Guidelines of the National Council for Hospice and Specialist Palliative Care Services (drafted by R Dunlop). *Clinical Guidelines for Pain Control*. London: National Council for Hospice and Specialist Palliative Care Services, 1994.

69 Walker VA, Hoskin PJ, Hanks GW et al. Evaluation of WHO analgesic guidelines for cancer pain in a hospital-based palliative care unit. *J Pain Symp Management* 1988; **3(3)**: 145–9.

70 Takeda F. Results of field-testing in Japan of the WHO draft interim guidelines of relief of cancer pain. *Pain Clin* 1986; **1**: 83–9.

71 Schug SA, Zech D, Dorr U. Cancer pain management according to WHO analgesic guidelines. *J Pain Symp Management* 1990; **5(1)**: 27–32.

72 Portenoy RK. Adjuvant analgesics in pain management. In *Oxford Textbook of Palliative Medicine* (eds D Doyle, GWC Hanks, N MacDonald). Oxford: Oxford Univeristy Press, 1993, pp. 229–44.

73 Pace V. The use of non-steroidal anti-inflammatory drugs in cancer. *Palliat Med* 1995; **9**: 273–86.

74 Twycross RG, Lack SA. *Control of alimentary symptoms in far advanced cancer*. Edinburgh: Churchill Livingstone, 1986.

75 Ventafridda V, Ripamonti C, Sbanotto A *et al.* Mouth care. In *Oxford Textbook of Palliative Medicine* (eds D Doyle, GWC Hanks, N MacDonald). Oxford: Oxford University Press, 1993, pp. 434–7.

76 Hanratty J, Higginson I (eds). *Palliative Care in Terminal Illness*. Oxford: Radcliffe Medical Press, 1994.

77 Regnard C, Ahmedzai S. Dyspnoea in advanced nonmalignant disease – a flow diagram. *Palliat Med* 1991; **5**: 56–60.

78 Johnson I, Patterson S. Drugs used in combination in the syringe driver – a survey of hospice practice. *Palliat Med* 1992; **6**: 125–30.

79 Baines M, Sykes N. Gastrointestinal symptoms. In *The management of terminal malignant disease* (eds C Saunders, N Sykes). 3rd edn. London: Edward Arnold, 1993, pp. 63–76.

80 Regnard C, Comiskey M. Nausea and vomiting in advanced cancer – a flow diagram. *Pall Med* 1992; **6(2)**: 146–51.

81 World Health Organization. *Targets for health for all – targets in support of a European strategy for health promotion*. Copenhagen: WHO, 1985.

82 Maguire P, Faulkner A. Communicating with cancer patients: 1 Handling bad news and difficult questions. *Br Med J* 1988; **297**: 907–9.

83 Maguire P, Faulkner A. Communicating with cancer patients: 2 Handling uncertainty, collusion, and denial. *Br Med J* 1988; **297**: 972–4.

84 Parkes CM. Home or hospital? Terminal care as seen by surviving spouses. *J Roy Coll Gen Practit* 1978; **28**: 19–30.

85 Higginson I, Wade A, McCarthy M. Palliative care: views of patients and their families. *Br Med J* 1990; **301**: 277–81.

86 Lunt B. A comparison of hospice care for terminally ill cancer patients and their families. Final report. Research funded under grant DHSS JR/121/692, 1986.

87 Addington-Hall JM, MacDonald L, Anderson H *et al.* Randomised controlled trial of effects of coordinating care for terminally ill cancer patients. *Br Med J* 1992; **305**: 1317–22.

88 Bowling A. Mortality after bereavement: a review of the literature on survival periods and factors affecting survival. *Soc Sci Med* 1987; **24(2)**: 117–24.

89 Bereavement. In *Oxford Textbook of Palliative Medicine* (eds D Doyle, GWC Hanks, N MacDonald). Oxford: Oxford University Press, 1993.

90 Bromberg M, Higginson I. Bereavement follow-up: what do support teams actually do? *J Palliat Care* 1996; **12(1)**: 12–17.

91 Wilkes E. Terminal cancer at home. *Lancet* 1965; **i**: 799–801.

92 Wilkes E. Dying now. *Lancet* 1984; **i**: 950–2.

93 Cartwright A, Hockey L, Anderson JL. *Life before death*. London: Routledge & Kegan Paul, 1973.

94 Parkes CM. Terminal care: evaluation of in-patient service at St Christopher's Hospice. Part I. Views of surviving spouse on effects of the service on the patient. *Postgrad Med J*, 1979; **55**: 517–22.

95 Mills M, Davis HTO, Macrae W. Care of dying patients in hospital. *Br Med J* 1994; **309**: 583–6.

96 Bowling A, Cartwright A. *Life after a death. A study of the elderly widowed*. London: Tavistock, 1982.

97 Maguire P. Monitoring the quality of life in cancer patients and their relatives. In *Cancer: assessment and monitoring*. London: Churchill Livingstone, 1980, pp. 40–52.

98 Ward AWM. Terminal care in malignant disease. *Soc Sci Med* 1974; **8**: 413–20.

99 Parkes CM. Terminal care: home, hospital, or hospice? *Lancet* 1985; **i**: 155–7.

100 Townsend J, Frank A, Fermont D *et al.* Terminal cancer care and patients' preference for place of death: a prospective study. *Br Med J* 1990; **301**: 415–17.

101 Dunlop R *et al.* Preferred versus actual place of death: a hospital palliative care support team study. *Palliat Med* 1989; **3**: 197–201.

102 Hinton J. Which patients with terminal cancer admitted from home care? *Palliat Med* 1994; **8**: 197–210.

103 Seale CF. What happens in hospices: a review of research evidence. *Soc Sci Med* 1989; **28(6)**: 551–9.

104 Kane RL, Klein SJ, Bernstein L *et al.* Hospice role in alleviating the emotional stress of terminal patients and their families. *Medical Care* 1985; **23(3)**: 189–97.

105 Kane RL, Wales J, Bernstein L *et al.* A randomised trial of hospice care. *Lancet* 1984; **i**: 890–4.

106 Higginson I, McCarthy M. Evaluation of palliative care: steps to quality assurance? *Palliat Med* 1989; **3**: 267–74.

107 Greer DS, Mor V, Morris JN *et al.* An alternative in terminal care: results of the National Hospice Study. *J Chron Dis* 1986; **39**: 9–26.

108 Greer DS, Mor V, Sherwood S *et al.* National Hospice Study analysis plan. *J Chron Dis* 1983; **36(11)**: 737–80.

109 Mor V, Greer DS, Kastenbaum R (eds). *The Hospice Experiment*. Baltimore: John Hopkins University Press, 1988, pp. 88–108.

110 Mor V, Morris JN, Hiris J *et al.* The effect of hospice care on where patients die. In *The Hospice Experiment* (eds V Mor, DS Greer, R Kastenbaum). Baltimore: John Hopkins University Press, 1988, pp. 133–46.

111 Morris JN, Sherwood S, Wright SM *et al.* The last weeks of life: does hospice make a difference? In *The Hospice Experiment* (eds V Mor, DS Greer, R Kastenbaum). Baltimore: John Hopkins University Press, 1988, pp.109–32.

112 Parkes CM. Terminal care: evaluation of in-patient service at St Christopher's Hospice. Part II. Self-assessments of effects of the service on surviving spouses. *Postgrad Med J* 1979; **55**: 523–7.

113 Parkes CM, Parkes J. Hospice versus hospital care – re-evaluation after 10 years as seen by surviving spouses. *Postgrad Med J* 1984; **60**: 120–4.

114 Field D, Ahmedzai S, Biswas B. Care and information received by lay carers of terminally ill patients at the Leicestershire Hospice. *Palliat Med* 1992; **July 6(3)**: 237–45.

115 Mor V, Greer DS, Goldberg R. The medical and social service interventions of hospice and non-hospice patients. In *The Hospice Experiment* (eds V Mor, DS Greer, R Kastenbaum). Baltimore: John Hopkins University Press, 1988.

116 Kidder D. The impact of hospice on the health-care costs of terminal cancer patients. In *The Hospice Experiment* (eds V Mor, DS Greer, R Kastenbaum). Baltimore: John Hopkins University Press, 1988, pp. 48–68.

117 Kidder D. Hospice services and cost savings in the last weeks of life. In *The Hospice Experiment* (eds V Mor, DS Greer, R Kastenbaum). Baltimore: John Hopkins University Press, 1988, pp. 69–87.

118 Hill F, Oliver C. Hospice – the cost of in-patient care. *Hlth Trnd* 1984; **16**: 9–11.

119 Hill F, Oliver C. Hospice – an update on the cost of patient care. *Hlth Trnd* 1988; **20**: 83–7.

120 Smith AM, Eve A, Sykes NP. Palliative care services in Britain and Ireland 1990 – an overview. *Palliat Med* 1992; **6**: 277–91.

121 Johnson I, Rogers C, Biswas B *et al.* What do hospices do? A survey of hospices in the United Kingdom and Republic of Ireland. *Br Med J* 1990; **300**: 791–3.

122 Kirkham S, Davis M. Bed occupancy, patient throughput and size of independent hospice units in the UK. *Palliat Med* 1992; **6**: 47–53.

123 Working Group of the Research Unit, Royal College of Physicians. Palliative care: guidelines for good practice and audit measures. *J R Coll Phys London* 1991; **25(4)**: 325–8.

124 Harper R, Ward A, Westlake L *et al. Good Practice in Terminal Care. Some standards and guidelines for hospice inpatient units and day hospices.* Sheffield: Department of Community Medicine, University of Sheffield Medical School, Beech Hill Road, 1988.

125 RCN Dynamic Quality Improvement Programme. *Standards of care for palliative nursing.* London: Royal College of Nursing, 1993.

126 Cancer Relief Macmillan Fund. *Organisational standards for palliative care.* London: Cancer Relief Macmillan Fund, 1994.

127 Ward AWM. Home care services – an alternative to hospices? *Comm Med* 1987; **9(1)**: 47–54.

128 Zimmer JG, Groth-Juncker A, McCusker J. Effects of a physician-led home care team on terminal care. *J Am Ger Soc* 1984; **32(4)**: 288–93.

129 Hughes SL, Cummings J, Weaver F *et al.* A randomized trial of the cost effectiveness of VA hospital-based home care for terminally ill. *Hlth Serv Res* 1992; **26(6)**: 801–17.

130 Cox K, Bergen A, Norman I. Exploring consumer views of care provided by the Macmillan nurse using the critical incident technique. *J Adv Nurs* 1993; **18**: 408–15.

131 Parkes CM. Terminal care: evaluation of an advisory domiciliary service at St Christopher's Hospice. *Postgrad Med J* 1980; **56**: 685–9.

132 Ventafridda V, De Conno F, Vigano A *et al.* Comparison of home and hospital care of advanced cancer patients. *Tumori* 1989; **75**: 619–25.

133 Creek LV. A homecare hospice profile: description, evaluation, and cost analysis. *J Family Practice* 1982; **14(1)**: 53–8.

134 Higginson I, McCarthy M. Measuring symptoms in terminal cancer: are pain and dyspnoea controlled? *J Roy Soc Med* 1989; **82**: 1761–4.

135 Seale C. Death from cancer and death from other causes: the relevance of the hospice approach. *Palliat Med* 1991; **5**: 12–19.

136 Hughes SL, Cummings J, Weaver F *et al.* A randomised controlled trial of VA hospital-based home care for the terminally ill. *Hlth Serv Res* 1992; **26(6)**: 801–17.

137 Tramarin A, Milocchi F, Tolley K *et al.* An economic evaluation of home-care assistance for AIDS patients: a pilot study in a town in northern Italy. *AIDS* 1992; **6(11)**: 1377–83.

138 Jones RVH. Teams and terminal cancer at home: do patients and carers benefit? *J Interprofess Care* 1993; **7(3)**: 239–44.

139 Irvine B. Development in palliative nursing in and out of the hospital setting. *Br J Nurs* 1993; **2(4)**: 218–24.

140 Griffin J. *Dying with dignity.* London: Office of Health Economics, 1991, pp. 4–45.

141 Theis S, Deitrick E. Respite Care: A community needs survey. *J Comm Hlth Nurs* 1987; **4(2)**: 85–92.

142 Johnson IS. The Marie Curie/St Luke's Relative Support Scheme: a home care services for relatives of the terminally ill. *J Adv Nurs* 1988; **13**: 565–70.

143 Koffman J, Higginson I. *Evaluation of a new hospice at home scheme.* London: Department of Public Health, Kensington, Chelsea and Westminster Health Authority, 1994.

144 Anand JK, Pryor GA. Hospital at home. *Hlth Trends* 1989; **21**: 46–8.

145 Higginson I, Webb D, Lessof L. Reducing beds for patients with advanced cancer. *Lancet* 1994; **344(8919)**: 409.

146 Cartwright A. Social class differences in health and care in the year before death. *J Epidem Comm Hlth* 1992; **46**: 54–7.

147 McCusker J, Stoddard AM. Effects of expanding home care program for the terminally ill. *Med Care* 1987; **B25(5)**: 373–84.

148 Butters E, Higginson I, George R *et al.* Palliative care for people with HIV/AIDS: views of patients, carers and providers. *AIDS Care* 1993; **5(1)**: 105–16.

149 Butters E, Higginson I, George R *et al.* Assessing the symptoms, anxiety and practical needs of HIV/AIDS patients receiving palliative care. *Qual Life Res* 1992; **1(1)**: 47–51.

150 Moss V. Patient characteristics, presentation and problems encountered in advanced AIDS in a hospice setting – review. *Palliat Med* 1991; **5**: 112–16.

151 East Anglian Regional Health Authority. *A Quality Framework for the Dying and Bereaved.* East Anglian Regional Health Authority. October 1992.

152 Finlay I, Wilkinson C, Gibbs C. Planning palliative care services. *Hlth Trnd* 1992; **24(4)** 139–41.

153 Haines A, Booroff A. Terminal care at home: perspective from general practice. *Br Med J* 1986; **292(6527)**: 1051–3.

154 Winget C, Higginson I. Palliative care – questionnaire survey of local general practitioners' views. In *Commissioning Specialist Palliative Care Services* (eds I Higginson, R Bush, P Jenkins, M Collins). London: Kensington & Chelsea and Westminster Health Commissioning Agency, 1994.

155 Copperman H. Domiciliary hospice care: a survey of general practitioners. *J R Coll Gen Practit* 1988; **38(314)**: 411–13.

156 Chambers E, Oakhill A, Cornish J *et al.* Terminal care at home for children with cancer. *Br Med J* 1989; **298**: 937–40.

157 Chambers T. Hospices for children? *Br Med J* 1987; **294**: 1309–10.

158 Higginson I, Bush R, Jenkins P *et al.* Commissioning specialist palliative care services. London: Kensington & Chelsea and Westminster Health Commissioning Agency, 1994.

159 Barnet Local Medical Committee. *Palliative care in Barnet – a guide for general practitioners and practice staff.* London: Department of Public Health, Barnet Health Commissioning Agency, 1993.

160 Ford GR, Pincherle G. Arrangements for terminal care in the NHS (especially those for cancer patients). *Hlth Trnd* 1978; **10**: 73–6.

161 Nicholas A, Frankenberg R. *Towards a strategy for palliative care - a needs assessment for Nottingham Health.* Nottingham: Department of Public Health, Nottingham Health, 1992.

162 Welsh Health Planning Forum. *Pain, discomfort and palliative care.* Cardiff: The Welsh Office NHS Directorate, 1992.

163 Robbins M, Jackson P. *Somerset study of patients and carers.* Bristol: Health Care Evaluation Unit, Department of Epidemiology and Public Health Medicine, University of Bristol, 1993.

164 Rutman D, Parke B. Palliative care needs of residents families and staff in long term care facilities. *J Palliat Care* 1992; **8(2)**: 23–9.

165 Murphy D, Bahr R, Kelly J *et al.* A needs assessment survey of HIV-infected patients. *West Indian Med J* 1992; **Jun**: 291–5.

166 Kincade J, Powers R. An assessment of palliative care needs in a tertiary care hospital. *QRB* 1984; **August**, 230–37.

167 Barnett M, McCarthy M. Identification of terminally-ill patients in the community. In *1986 International Symposium on Pain Control* (ed. D Doyle). London: Royal Society of Medicine: 78–80. (123 in International Symposium Series), 1987.

168 Neale B, Clark D, Heather P. *Purchasing palliative care: a review of the policy and research literature.* Sheffield: Trent Palliative Care Centre, 1993.

169 Zalot GN. Planning a regional palliative care services network. *J Palliat Care* 1989; **5(1)**: 42–6.

170 Robbins MA, Frankel SJ. Palliative care: what needs assessment. *Palliat Med* 1995; **9**: 287–93.

171 Addington-Hall JM, McCarthy M. Audit methods: views of the family after the death. In *Clinical audit in palliative care* (ed. I Higginson). Oxford: Radcliffe Medical Press, 1993, pp. 88–100.

172 National Council for Hospice and Specialist Palliative Care Services. Needs Assessment for Hospice and Specialist Palliative Care Services: from philosophy to contracts. *Occasional paper 4.* London: National Council for Hospice and Specialist Palliative Care Services, 1993.

173 Working party on clinical guidelines in palliative care (drafted by I Higginson). Outcome measures in palliative care. London: National Council for Hospice and Specialist Palliative Care Services, 1995.

174 Bowling A. *Measuring health. A review of quality of life measurement scales.* Milton Keynes: Open University, 1991.

175 Katz S. The science of quality of life. *J Chron Dis* 1987; **40(6)**: 449–63.

176 Quality of life. In *Oxford Textbook of Palliative Medicine* (eds D Doyle, GWC Hanks, N MacDonald). Oxford: Oxford University Press, 1993.

177 Department of Health. *Pressure sores and key quality indicator*. Heywood: Health Publication Unit, 1993.

178 Higginson I, McCarthy M. Validity of a measure of palliative care – comparison with a quality of life index. *Palliat Med* 1994; **8(4)**: 282–90.

179 Higginson I. A community schedule. In *Clinical Audit in Palliative Care* (ed. I Higginson). Oxford: Radcliffe Medical Press, 1993 pp. 34–47.

180 Bruera E, Macdonald S. The Edmonton Symptom Assessment System. In *Clinical Audit in Palliative Care* (ed. I Higginson). Oxford: Radcliffe Medical Press, 1993, pp. 61–77.

181 de Haes JCJM, van Knippenbery FCE, Neijt. Measuring psychological and physical distress in cancer patients: structure and application of the Rotterdam Symptom Checklist. *Br J Cancer* 1990; **62**: 1034–8.

182 Aaronson NK, Ahmedzai S, Bergman B *et al*. The European Organisation for Research and Treatment of Cancer QLQ-C30: a quality of life instrument for use in international clinical trials in oncology. *J Nat Cancer Inst* 1993; **85(5)**: 365–75.

183 Zigmond AS, Snaith RP. The Hospital Anxiety and Depression Scale. *Acta Psychiatrica Scandinavica* 1983; **67**: 361–70.

184 Trent Hospice Audit Group. *Palliative Care Core Standards: a multidisciplinary approach*. Nightingale Macmillan Continuing Care Unit, Trinity Street, Derby, 1992.

185 Dixon P, Heaton J, Long A *et al*. Reviewing and applying the SF-36. *Outcomes briefing* (UK Clearing House on Health Outcomes) 1994; **4**: 3–25.

186 Hill S, Harris U. Assessing the outcome of health care for the older person in community settings: should we use the SF-36? *Outcomes briefing* (UK Clearing House on Health Outcomes) 1994; **4**: 26–7.

187 Karnofsky DA, Abelmann WH, Craver LF *et al*. The use of nitrogen mustards in the palliative treatment of carcinoma. *Cancer* 1948; **I**: 634–56.

188 Melzack R. The McGill pain questionnaire: major properties and scoring methods. *Pain* 1975; **I**: 277–99.

189 Maguire P, Selby P. Assessing quality of life in cancer patients. *Br J Cancer* 1989; **60(3)**: 437–40.

190 Fallowfield L. *The quality of life. The missing measurement in health care*. London: Souvenir Press, 1990.

191 Wilkin D, Hallam L, Doggett MA. *Measures of need and outcome for primary health care*. Oxford: Oxford University Press, 1992.

192 Bowling A. *Measuring disease*. Milton Keynes: Open University Press, 1995.

193 Slevin ML. Quality of life: philosophical question or clinical reality? *Br Med J* 1992; **305**: 466–9.

194 Spitzer WO. State of science 1986: Quality of life and functional status as target variables for research. *J Chron Dis* 1987; **40(6)**: 465–71.

195 Thomas VJ, Rose FD. Ethnic differences in the experience of pain. *Soc Sci Med* 1991; **32(9)**: 1063–6.

196 Clarke M, Finlay I, Campbell I. Cultural boundaries in care. *Palliat Med* 1991; **5**: 63–5.

197 Cassidy S. Emotional distress in terminal cancer. *J Royal Society Med* 1986; **79**: 717–20.

198 Goddard M. The role of economics in the evaluation of hospice care. *Hlth Policy* 1989; **13**: 19–34.

199 Higginson I, Butters E, Murphy F *et al*. Computer database for palliative care. *Lancet* 1992; **340**: 243.

200 Higginson I, Butters E, Murphy F *et al*. Audit experience: using a data base to audit care. In *Clinical Audit in Palliative Care* (ed. I Higginson). Oxford: Radcliffe Medical Press, 1993, pp. 156–67.

201 National Council for Hospice and Palliative Care Services and The Hospice Information Service. *Data manual. Minimum data sets project*. London: National Council for Hospice and Palliative Care Services, 1995.

202 Department of Public Health. *1993 Annual Public Health Report*. London: Kensington, Chelsea and Westminster Health Commissioning Agency, 1993.

Acknowledgements

I am very grateful to a number of individuals who have provided me with help and useful suggestions in the preparation of this document. In particular I would like to thank Dr Derek Doyle, Dr Gill Ford, Dr Julia Addington-Hall, Dr Andrew Stevens, Dr James Raftery and the external referees for their helpful comments on earlier drafts of this document; my colleagues in Kensington & Chelsea and Westminster Health Authority (KCWHA) with whom I developed a palliative needs assessment, which formed the pilot for much of the work outlined here, and in particular Robina Bush, Paul Jenkins, Mary Collins and Catherine Winget and colleagues in the local hospices and specialist palliative care services, who provided helpful advice and comments on the KCWHA needs assessment – Dr Anne Naysmith, Dr Philip Jones, Dr Joe Chamberlain and Dr Rob George. I would like to thank Professor Michael Clarke and colleagues in Leicester for sharing information on the epidemiologically based needs assessment for the elderly, which they were preparing and which helped me formulate some of my ideas. Finally I am indebted to Franky Eynon and Sarah Scutt for their help in preparing the manuscript.

Index